Psychic Ability, Clairvoyant Powers

Mediumship   Attunement

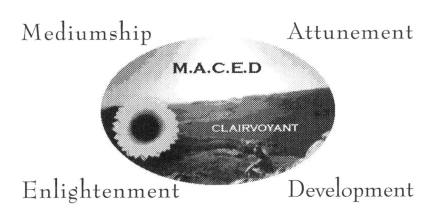

M.A.C.E.D

CLAIRVOYANT

Enlightenment   Development

Joe Brown

PUBLISH AMERICA

PublishAmerica
Baltimore

ISBN: 1-4241-5305-0 (softcover)
ISBN: 978-1-4489-6039-2 (hardcover)
PUBLISHED BY PUBLISHAMERICA, LLLP
www.publishamerica.com
Baltimore

Printed in the United States of America

This book is lovingly dedicated
to my dear friend
Margaret Young.

Contents

Preface

This book is written for an individual or group of people who would like to become aware of and develop their psychic ability for further development of their hidden talents. The contents and meditations are not written for skeptics but for a person in need of soul searching and learning more about life on the other side, the spirit world.

The chapters are short, condensed, intense and very informative; they are not filled with a lot of nothingness. It contains straight to the point information to give the awareness needed for a better understanding of the psychic gift and inner connections with the God source while opening a channel for clairvoyant insight and ability.

What you read and learn from here are from personal experiences I've had over a period of years. As I share them with you you'll be capable of reaching the spirit world by going within to find that contact which you so desire.

This is a beginner's guide written in a simple format and easily understood. It's also an introduction to Spiritualism, although you don't have to be of the Spiritualism religion to advance spiritually or have the ability to contact those that has passed over. Each religion teaches of an afterlife but being in a group that demonstrates it would be beneficial to you as those that are, are of the same mind. Spiritualism is a religion, science and philosophy that demonstrate proof of survival of physical death.

The contents are written in a way that I would have liked to have found when I was a beginner. Personally I feel there are great Mediums out there but they have not yet put their teachings on paper. I too continue to learn each day and keep an open mind for a greater understanding of spirit.

For the reader who doesn't have an interest in developing his skills, the information and true ghost stories will provide you with enlightenment. As you continue to read let the sub-consciousness of your mind be the judge of any inner feelings dealing with an afterlife. Your intuitive knowingness will provide you with a positive aspect of immortality.

As a student or a new Medium we have a responsibility to be honest and serious in our approach to mediumship and the development of it.

On the other hand as a spiritualist person on a spiritual path we come to realize that communication with Spirit Entities brings joy and upliftment for those who seek that special communion.

Try hard to be perfect in your gifted ability even though it will bring you down a peg or two with certain challenges. Strive to possess that spiritual energy that'll keep you going so you'll become stronger.

Be your own worst judge, as I am, because by being so you'll gain insight and knowingness. React wisely and learn from experiences of your past gains and unwanted failures.

We start life as students and become aware of our surroundings as we grow through spiritual awareness, even through hardships and yet we continue to learn. In our silence there's much wisdom; therefore by using intuition and guidance from the higher source we connect and communicate.

Spiritualism is a loving religion, as many others, which has potential growth, understanding and its practise is focused towards a loving perspective.

We need to strive on a day-to-day basis to be a better person so that communication with our friends from the other side will develop to perfection.

When you're new to meditation and mediumship you'll often wonder if there will ever be any contact from spirit strong enough to make you aware of it. Just remember to give yourself the necessary time it takes to go within and be able to seek this awareness. When you make that first contact you'll finally recognize that it hasn't been that far away from the beginning. Spirit is compelled to seek out such contacts as well as we're seeking to make that contact with them.

As you develop and learn, please have respect for your fellow man and treat him with dignity regardless of race, colour or creed. They're all a part of our daily lives and God's universe. We're all special and we're all unique; love heals far beyond any other means. Togetherness in harmony means world peace; moreover let's enlighten our souls and become aware that happiness is created. Create it and live peacefully within it.

The most important relationship you'll discover is how to communicate with your spirit guides. They'll become much more important once you become aware of and how to sense them, as you continue to unfold that tremendous power you have within.

You'll eventually rely heavily on your guides, guardians and angels, as they are all teachers and helpers from the god source. They're always with you guiding and helping in many ways you're not even aware of. They're surrounding you with so much love; if not already you'll eventually feel their protective energy, especially when you're in great need of spiritual or angelic assistance.

Your soul will beckon for extra awareness, but the positive energy in life is right there within your own consciousness

Acknowledgement

Margaret Young, my dearest friend, has been an inspiration of brightness in my life for 20 years. Without her encouragement, love, caring and understanding I would not have gotten the proper insight that I needed to guide and lead me on this chosen path of God. Thank you for always being there when I knew I could lean on you at any time. Your continuous help, support and love have never faltered. You are an eternal friend.

Bonnie Houghton I thank you for your encouragement and the many hours of time shared with me to learn and develop our skills together. You have a wonderful gift and also able to contact the spirit world, there's no doubt that you'll be a very good Medium in time; I also thank God for having another reliable friend. Permission to use your children's picture is greatly appreciated. Love, peace and harmony will remain in our lives.

Jose Padial from Madrid, Spain and *Lyse LePage* from Toronto, Ontario, Canada. I thank for all your encouragement and the quick development you grasped from my knowledge and teachings. You're two of the first who sat with me to learn; I consider you to be two of my first so-called students. You both did exceptionally well and pressed forward to develop your abilities of which you're more that capable.

Rev. Doreen Bauld, Springdale Church, Scarborough, I

8

thank you for taking the time to read this book, my manuscript, and for giving me your advanced knowledge and insight into rewording some of the minor errors overlooked on my part. I would also like to thank you for accepting me in your paid closed development class and giving me the hands on opportunity to practice. You said you could fine-tune my abilities and you most certainly have. As time goes on I feel you'll be more than just another teacher, you'll be someone that I'll reflect back on with love and admiration. You've been very good as an introduction of advanced awareness towards my learning; I know you have much more to share and that many will greatly benefit from it.

Rev. Alva Folkes, The Fellowship of Spiritualists Church, Whitby, I thank you for also taking the time to read my book, my manuscript, and for sharing with me your great wisdom of world knowledge. You are one of the best Mediums I have ever met. I feel your capabilities succeed way beyond mediumship and that you're already on the road to a higher developed awareness. You have my blessings and God has done well with such a high-spirited lady such as yourself. Your time given to me was with unconditional love. I do appreciate all of your undivided attention and of all the free time and information you gave so willingly. You encourage your students and church members to advance in their spiritual growth and you show them the way if needed. You've became a wonderful friend as well as someone I look up to and admire.

See more of Reverend Alva's capabilities Chapter four, Reincarnation.

Ms. Sharon Kerr I thank you for getting me in touch with one of my best advisors, Rev. Alva Folkes. Because you introduced me to her my spiritual advancement did not remain at a standstill. Rev. Alva has taken me that extra step towards my educational development, which was my next step of spiritual growth.

Rev. Judy Merrill, Spiritualist Church of Wisdom, Scarborough, I thank you for accepting me in the middle of the year of your closed development class; you gave me a first start when others wouldn't. I would also like to thank you for granting me permission to use a quote from Elizabeth Harris's book, 'Spiritualism— A way of life'.

May God Bless Each and Everyone

Complimentary Appraisals

I remember a lot when I was at your home, and I am so thankful for your interest in order to guide me, which has brought me ever more happiness. I try to follow the meditation exercises everyday,

I know for sure that you are going be an outstanding medium and the Reverend at the church has realised this fact, therefore she doesn't want to let you go. Being in the medical filed helps in this matter because you are in constant personal contact with the emotions of people out of material and sometimes deceiving feelings from other environments. I considered myself a really lucky person for having met you, I'm so proud of it.

Jose Padial, Madrid, Spain

Your book is a perfect personal introduction to God and to Spiritualism for the inquiring mind. It gives a gentle, but direct guidance to the beginner. You are definitely on the right path. You do have a great talent and you're where you belong. Go forward! You are taking giant steps as the past has been small steppingstones to the 'now.' Continue as always to follow the path that best suits your own personal and Spiritual growth. Our time together in discussion and meditation has helped me greatly in my own Spiritual awakening and growth. For this, I will always be grateful to you. You inspired me and gave me the direction at the time I needed it most. You have become a dear and treasured friend. Thank you! Love and Light.

Bonnie Houghton, Etobicoke, Ont. Ca.

I have to say that I think there is a very great future for you in the spiritual realm—you have a great gift and there are people out there who will help you to become very well known in the quite near future and I shall be very proud to say, oh yes, I've known him for a long time! I guess that from your experiences it is exhausting, but think what joy you will be able to bring to others.

Honor Kay, England, UK

"When the heart and mind are open, Spirit is willing to communicate. This book is a good example of how to learn basic meditation without a formal teacher."

Reverend Alva Folkes, Whitby, Ontario Ca.

Your story written about God is very moving, it takes a long time for someone to reach a level were they feel such peace and understanding about our spiritual connection with a higher being. Using your own true-life experiences makes it real for others, shows them the strength of prayer and belief. It moved me very much. I take great comfort in your daily prayer each day and those written words from you, although I do not believe it is a story, it is something else that describes your thoughts you have recorded. I believe that you are following your destiny and are reaching the focal point of your life. I am so proud of you.

Dorothy Mary Senior, Winterland, Newfoundland, Ca.

Your private circle on Wednesday evenings is very interesting. I still have goose bumps when I think about my experience (holding hands with my spirit guide). Thank you. Your circles will do well; I'm sure of that, they have you as a tutor! You are very good at teaching and I have no doubt that your book will sell well. Your new students and I both have no idea where we are going when it comes to spiritual messaging. As for me lately, I'm learning to connect with the spirit world a lot more quickly. Your teaching circle will be a very popular event. I know we will do well because we have a good coach, you.

Lyse LePage, Toronto, Ontario, Ca.

This is great, I'm glad that you've joined a private circle as well as teach and I shall look forward with interest as to your progress. All experience is valuable, and anything you do to expand your horizons is for your benefit for the sake of helping others.

Margaret Young, Mississauga, Ont. Ca.

It was a real pleasure reading your manuscript. I really did enjoy it. I realize that you put your heart and soul into this. I felt that a lot of compassion and honesty went into your writing.

Kathryon, New Market, Ontario

It was a real pleasure reading your manuscript. I really did enjoy it. I realize that you put your heart and soul into this. I felt

that a lot of compassion and honesty went into your writing.
Tony (Fellow development classmate) Mississauga, Ontario,
Canada

Your book is great. I have a hard time putting it down. When I read the part about past lives I was trilled about what I was reading.
Juanita Parsons (development classmate) Pickering, Ontario,
Canada

I've made a vow to myself that I would help others find their way and develop if the need arises. It can be frustrating when you know it's there and unable to carry it any further. I've always gotten positive feedback and encouragement from my own circle members. We all need this in our progression as it always makes us strive to better ourselves and want to help someone new with their development.
J.A. Brown, Author

You, as a Medium

You're very capable of working with your psych and have the clairvoyant gifts that you see many mediums possess, henceforth becoming a Medium. This is a perfect guidebook for beginners to help make that first contact with the spirit world.

Just how do you accomplish a spirit contact and know that's what really happened? How do you retain this wonderful ability once you have beaten the odds and finally connected with spirit? Question after question; I had many which were diverted or didn't seem to get any direct answers for. You don't have to put as much effort into this as I because this book is all you'll ever need to accomplish what you so desire to start on the right path and to explore this beautiful gift from God.

Psychic abilities are within us all; clairvoyant powers are within some of us but one need only to know how to tap into it. Back in biblical times spirits appeared to many, natural law hasn't changed. Even to this day it's happening all the time but people are made to think that it's of their imagination. Life in the material world is all about learning, learning to live peacefully and to be totally connected to the source of your being that which is connected to the Divine.

Our subconscious mind works best and has more power when working with symbols; with most on a spiritual path one may find that they'll grasp the meaning of the message more quickly, then that of another means such as psychometry, once awareness and interruption has been mindful. As you progress with this method it opens doors for the perceptual shifts that are necessary for your growth and future development. One may not realize it but there's a barrier between you and your world, the world as you know it and the world beyond the material, the spirit world. Understand that to be whom you really are you must attune to break through this barrier for soul progression and develop from **Psychic Ability to Clairvoyant Powers.**

Being a Medium is not always a bed of roses. 99% of the time it seems that way but the other 1% is what you have to be most aware of. That one percent deals with an incorrect message that you rolled over and over in your mind and didn't stick with your first impressions. Don't fight against spirit, listen to what's being said, be fully aware of what's being shown and decipher its meaning and create the message from the contents given. When you become good at spiritual contact and you're unsure, go back in and ask again, and again, until the feeling is definitely right. When you're new to this give what you get, relate what you see, sense and feel, and nothing else. Don't create a message if you're not totally sure of what you sense. I stress this once again; give what you get. The most important information I can give you is; have faith in yourself and strive to be the best you can. Listen to your inner self, that small inner voice, and stick with your first impressions. Spirit won't steer you in the wrong direction.

Never give a negative message. If one comes through soften the blow and rearrange it so that the receiver will be aware, or don't give it at all. If you do choose to relay it please give some guidance of where spirit would like them to go with it. Never leave anyone in the lurch with something they'll worry about for a long time to come. Always consider and respect this.

Some Mediums become very good at spiritual contact; they go into business for themselves and rely on it as a second income. Some use it as a full time occupation. Some may charge for a reading but one should not focus on this for personal gain. There's a power source much greater then that of your own and eventually you'll come to realize what lies beyond this existence.

I have had several contacts with the spirit world prior to my development that scared the heck out of me as they were so abrupt. I didn't know how to interpret the message that was meant to come across; you'll read about some of them in chapter eleven. Now as I look back I can interpret every one of them. So if you have a friend or know of someone who has had several contacts with a so-called ghost or ghosts, encourage them to seek out that information; where else better to find it than in this book or in an advanced development circle. The teacher, the leader or the Medium will most likely have the answers. Don't be afraid to ask no matter how silly it may seem to you. Sometimes a phone call will get better results other than trying to get to speak with them personally while there are so many other people around during a gathering.

If you're interested in joining a development circle I advise you to go to one of the services where the Reverend-in-charge is chairing the service and doing the clairvoyance. Any organization is as good as its leader, so therefore a church is as good as its head chaplain. Listen to the messages given; get a feel if they're actually from spirit or it's something personal that they know about that person from the start. The only way to determine if one is in contact with the spirit world is to attend until you finally get proof of a passed loved one that is concrete in your mind or you can get its accuracy validated. Either right then and there or if you can't recall a contact, investigate; you may have to inquire and seek some information from an elder member of your family. Nevertheless, once it's verified you'll know you've gone to the right place.

A little insight for the curious and the believer: A good or 'High Quality Medium' don't ask questions when relaying spirit messages or doing a personal reading.

A Daily Prayer

God, Great Divine, our creator
Descend upon my heart, here on earth and make my energy flow
Help me with my weakness; give me inner peace and strength
Direct me to give love, as your will desires
Give me comfort from the Angels you so lovingly gave to watch over me
Cleanse my soul and make it pure
Let my heart beat of love for my fellow man
Strengthen my Mind, Body and Spirit so that I may be a better person
I will passionately love you as Your Angels do
The dove descended from your eternal light will set my heart aflame
You have entered into my soul and I feel your blessings.
Thank You.
Amen

We Believe In:

1: The Fatherhood of God.
2: The Brotherhood of Man.
3: Communion of Spirits and the Ministry of Angels.
4: The continuous existence of the Human Soul.
5: Personal Responsibility.
6: Compensation and Retribution hereafter
for all the good and evil deeds done on earth.
7: Eternal Progress open to every soul.

The seven Principles of the Spiritualist Churches
Followed by its faithful members.

Oh Creator of all, permeating the entire Universe,
Honour and Glory to Thee.
Your Divine Love pervades, is within and blesses all.
Your natural Law guides on the physical and spiritual planes.
Your Grace and Spiritual Energy sustains us.
Abundance prevails.
All life is growth, so we judge not ourselves or others.
Lead us on our paths, inspire us and protect us with your White
Light.
Life and Love are continuous, for all is God and perfection.

*Affirmative Prayer said at divine services in some
Spiritualist Churches.*

Chapter One
Mediumship

God's Listening

In earnest prayer the holy stream flows
Where warn devotions dwell the theme sweetly glows
Blessings desired grasps upward gaze
Celestial love eloquence of praise
Voices of sweetness heard by your ears
God's heart rejoiced then dried bitter tears
Spirit ascends utterance from out there
God lovingly accepts the comprehend prayer.

Mediumship or any event that appears to be unaccounted for by conventional physical, biological, or psychological theories, I feel it has to do with extrasensory perception (ESP), or the acquiring of information through nonsensory means, such as the thought process. In most opinions it would be called Spiritual Contact from the other side. What you'll be learning here is Mental Mediumship while dealing with your psyche, concentrating on your sixth sense and working with clairvoyance, clairaudience and clairsentience. Physical phenomena is explained but a development teacher is required for advancement after learning and grasping all that's enclosed in this book, if interested.

Many of us have this ability and are able to connect with spirit through daily prayer and meditation. For instance, when you wake in the morning you feel somewhat rested, especially after a good night's sleep. But once you have a pleasant shower you feel invigorated and fresh anew. That's what actually happens when you have a good deep session of meditation, you feel cleansed once you willingly open your senses to the spirit world; you'll feel refreshed beyond belief. Psychical connection is made possible through this means.

A medium is a person who uses their psychic abilities to communicate with people who had died, in a material sense, that are very much alive in the spirit world. They are called mediums because they're in the middle of a three-way communication for example: 1. from a spirit, 2. to the medium, which passes on or relates a message, such as proof of survival to; 3. the recipient. The communicators can be relatives, friends, guides or someone in spirit who knows someone connected to the recipient and wishes to get a message to the recipient.

There are many different kinds of mediumship and most mediums use a variety of gifts in their work. Each medium is unique in their way of connecting with the spirit world. Even though they may be trained in the same basic techniques; the way they work is based on how their personal spirit guides are able to work most effectively with them.

Mediumship helps ease the pain of those who are grieving for someone who has passed into spirit by proving that their loved ones are still alive, free from pain and wishing to communicate with those on earth. This information also helps to remove the fear of death. It teaches that we are spirit, temporarily using a physical body and that our spirit, the real individual, lives forever with the opportunity to keep evolving.

Making a spirit contact in a trance state is called channelling. A person who is able to channel is one who conveys thoughts or energy from a source believed to be outside the person's body or conscious mind, specifically One that speaks for non-physical beings or spirits.' Channelling is quite different from clairvoyance. Clairvoyance gives proof of survival of a personality after death and sometimes deals with related topics such as trance mediumship, haunting, apparitions and sometimes out-of-body experiences and so on.

There are two groups who investigate these phenomena, the Society Of Psychical Research, founded in England in 1882 and in the U.S. in 1884. Both groups continue to publish their findings up until today. This in itself is an example of scientific proof that an individual such as you or I could look into for personal satisfaction and peace of mind.

Many people are drawn to study more about life after death and try to develop their own 'psychic ability', which opens their minds to the spiritual laws that govern life. With this approach it helps many people to turn their lives around by helping them to find their own connection with God. This information will also assist you to recognize and hear your own inner voice (That small voice you often neglect or push aside) and provide you with the tools to fulfill your own spiritual destiny without fear.   .

Spiritualistic séances were held frequently back in the late 1800s and are still being preformed in certain individuals' homes even today. Spiritualism, as a religion, does not hold this in any given church that I'm aware of but to my knowledge some of them know and still participate in this activity on occasions in a private home. This has always been of interest to me and I now hold a private séance each time all of my students attend class.

My daughter, as a girl of about 10 years, was invited to a candle light séance held among fellow friends ranging from 10 to 15 year olds. One of them had read an article based on the supernatural and decided to gather his friends together one evening to perform what he had read, with him being the only male amongst them. As the time went on and the evening got very dark, they decided to sit around the table, held hands making a complete circle, with a candle burning in the centre as the only light source. I have no idea what chant or words were used to attract this phenomenal apparition but she said eventually a man of spirit did appear.

He was an old man with white hair, fairly hefty in size and dressed in ordinary daily attire. When my daughter saw this phenomenon she let out a scream that quickly broke the silence, scaring herself and the company of her friends half to death. She was terrified about what she saw as she didn't know or think that this was ever possible. This experience had opened new outlooks on life and death for her and made her wise never to participate in an unsupervised situation again, especially with amateurs who know nothing about the powers of spirit beyond the grave.

To this day she remembers that dark night, with the moon shining full circle. At the strike of midnight they called a man in spirit from his resting-place, only to frighten them but also to give proof that the soul does exist after the body has died. She now realizes that this way of spirit communication is more than capable of bringing a message of Love and Peace to those who wish to receive and are in need of a spiritual contact with a deceased loved one. When she finally related this to me, I did a little investigation. I found out that the house where they held the séance was once used as a large work shed. A man of similar stature as the apparition she had witnessed also used it as a small cottage during the summer. This cottage-shed was now made larger and converted into a permanent home by her friend's parents.

In my understanding mental manifestations, ESP, including telepathy is the direct transmission of messages, emotions, or other subjective states from one person to another without the use of any sensory channel of communication. Clairvoyance is a direct response to a physical object or event given through a past loved one. This is quite often without any sensory contact and precognition, or a non-inferential response to a future event.

The contents of verbal utterances by mental mediums are always welcome when it's a contact made with a loved one from the other side that we wanted to hear from. These phenomena can rarely be duplicated but taken as truth from word of mouth of the receiving medium, giving the message. This phenomenon occurs beyond the law of causality, which is one of the reasons that make this contact questionable by certain skeptics. This is accepted with total belief when the message has a text that only the person receiving understands. Sometimes it's verified immediately.

Since ancient times people have wondered about various so-called psychic experiences that seem to defy scientific explanation. Often these phenomena have been associated with communications with the so-called dead. Mediums that purport to mediate between the living and the dead were particularly popular in the 19th century. Often mediums will receive messages from a spirit contact while in trance or in a quiet meditation; their followers totally believed in their ability to do so. In recognizing this special gift they do sincerely believe that the delivered messages are from their deceased.

The ability to communicate with the dead or a past loved one has its happy and sad moments. I've been in a half trance state just recently and there was an entity using my arms. His spirit had tightened the muscles in my upper body in a vice like grip telling me that he's holding and hugging the lady I'm doing the reading for. I kept telling her this to appease the spirit but finally I had to tell this spirit to leave; he was physically and mentally exhausting me way beyond my means and capabilities of holding him at bay. She said it was probably out of guilt on his part by following his mother's negative influence and the decisions he made to appease her years ago while on the earth plane.

ESP actually underlies clairvoyance but most scientists don't believe that ESP exists. These scientists note that thousands of controlled studies have failed to show any evidence of psychical phenomena, and that no person has ever successfully demonstrated ESP for independent investigators. J.P. Rhine established a parapsychology lab about fifty years ago and he developed experiments that seemed to show that some people had remarkable ESP. Most scientists deny claims of clairvoyance because any substantial scientific evidence cannot support it, but verification of any given message proven to be true by the person receiving it is all that is needed by spiritualist believers and their followers. Despite these findings surveys indicate that a substantial portion of the public believes in ESP and Clairvoyance. Clairvoyance is a form of ESP which includes any ability to gain information by psychic means rather than through the physical senses. Clairvoyance from a trance medium or one in a deep meditation describes the objects or events that appear in his or her mind more clearly than a psychic or a fraudulent medium that is out there for personal gain and profit.

Patanjali says, *"Clairvoyance and telepathy are not the aim of Yoga practice, they are by-products of this practice. Cosmic Consciousness and universal penetration are the inherent nature of mind. Individual mind does not feel its cosmic form because of impurities. It is only when these impurities have been removed that the mind begins to feel cosmic penetration. This purity is achieved only through meditation and contemplation practice according to the classical systems of Yoga."*

Spiritualism has been practiced in one form or another since prehistoric times. Modem Spiritualism is the result of the 19th-century occurrences and research. About 1848 in the U.S. the older sister exploited Margaret and Kate Fox as alleged child mediums. This aroused sensational news stories that spurred the creation of a cult of Spiritualism. Although Margaret, as an adult, confessed to using tricks for some of the rapping's done, most of them were genuine. Plus, an American Medium, Andrew Jackson Davis was capable of performing certain intellectual feats when he was in trance that he could not perform normally. During this time period a British surgeon named James Braid came into the picture and provided a scientific explanation of mesmerism and thus helped to establish the modem technique of hypnosis.

So, all was not lost from past experiences of mediumship from some well known people. They had been remembered and written about so that those that hold an interest will also benefit from their experiences. Gifted mediums need more recognition and more publicity so that people like you and I will get a better insight into what is going on within us.

Clairaudient means the power or faculty of hearing something not present to the ear but regarded as having objective reality. Sometimes when you're in contact with spirit you'll hear different sounds like music, chimes, the sound of birds singing, the sound of a train, water falls and so on.

Clairsentience is the sensing you feel from spirit. You can actually sense a problem that this contact once had while alive or an actual illness causing his or her death. This is one way that this particular spirit can make itself known, by giving verification of something that only the receiver would know.

All of the above gives you more to work with in getting the message more correctly, providing you gain knowledge and learn all those capabilities.

Rev. John Golsby, an ordained minister in the state of New York, USA is a well-known Medium, he said, *"You are spirit, receiving a message from Spirit, to give to Spirit."* To verify his words look in the Holy Bible, in the book of John, Chapter 4 verse 24. Jesus said, *"God is spirit: and they that worship him must worship him in spirit and truth".*

Elizabeth Harris wrote a book called, 'Spiritualism, A way of life'. Let's review a short portion from it that verified my way of receiving and working as a beginner. She said, quoted from her book." *Spiritualists are experienced in spiritual attunement and receiving inspiration from the spirit world. We have perfected methods to do so."* She also said, 'When it comes to Spiritual connection through Meditation and *or Prayer, the guidelines are: We wait patiently for attunement to happen—we abstract ourselves from our environment— minimize light and sound—shut the eyes. In the darkness of closed eyes—we watch. In the silence—we listen. Settling comfortably—we feel. Thoughts and ideas will surge into our consciousness. If these thoughts and ideas prove to be inspirational, original, inventive then they are considered inspirational and* we *use them to create."*

If you haven't read this book, I highly recommend it. Seek it out and purchase it so that you may gain a better insight.

The verification I needed was received by attending a Spiritualist church and listening to lectures by some well-known mediums and also by reading the contents offered in her book.

Prepare yourself with a few minutes of silence prior giving any messages, whether it's within a circle or a private setting. Open yourself to the higher power of the universe and consciously allow the creative energy to move through you. You'll feel a radical spiritual-transformation taking place on a deeper level of consciousness when you connect with spiritual awareness.

This awareness is a creative spiritual power of the universe within us all. You'll get very good results from this exercise and some of your best messages from spirit come through more clearly by this practice. In time you won't need to meditate quite as long. You'll become aware of spirit much faster as you attune and develop.

This I had to achieve mostly on my own as I didn't get a lot of satisfaction from the answers I received from the many questions asked to those I felt could give me the proper solutions. I didn't consider those answers concrete guidance of creative enlightenment while I was on my quest of soul searching. I knew I had to take charge of my own development and put extra effort into becoming my own mediator. It seemed like everything was a big secret not to be shared. I turned to books, listened to my guides and that's where my development originated. I consider myself self-taught with the help of my Spirit Guides, Healing Guide and My Guardian Angel. Once I finally learned how to tap into my higher self and make a spirit connection I started to attend an open development circle for extra practice which defined a fine-tuning technique.

They say a picture says a thousand words. Ok, let's say there were 100 people looking at the same picture, all 100 people would have a different 1000 words, with some of them having a similar message but no one would have the exact same. When we start to see or visualize the images spirit is giving us for a particular sitter or a fellow circle member, *{one of a gathering of friends practicing clairvoyance and medium-ship,}* we'll know what that image means to us. So therefore you create a message from that. When that much is given Spirit will probably show you another image, you also know what that means to you, so therefore you create and give. Spirit is not going to give you something you can't totally understand. Spirit usually gives you visual images, scenes or pictures from which you are more then capable of creating your own 1000 words. This enables you to create the message that is to be given to the person you've focused on, or were drawn to by a higher source; it's called an inner intuitive knowingness. Your intuitive mind will have access to an infinite supply of information, knowledge and wisdom from the universal intelligent mind as you continue to rely on your guides. The more you trust and follow this inner voice the more you'll feel connected. The better connected you are the better you'll be able to make contact with a loved one with accuracy. Trust the feelings you get and act on it. If you need clarification go back and ask for it. It takes practice to hear and trust but in time more opportunities will open up for you as you grow more sensitive to your perception of spirit. Eventually you'll feel yourself flowing with the energy. Just trust in yourself when you go within to seek that inner knowledge of which you have already become aware. You know its there so trust in your own knowingness and don't hesitate to believe in yourself. The more you receive, the more you'll be able to give. Strengthen yourself so you'll be able to bring more power, creativity and love.

You'll become who you want to be and who you really are through giving yourself a time period and making meditation a part of your daily life. This process will help create an understanding within you and help develop your inner awareness. There's hard work involved but anything good that will come to you will be through hard work and perseverance. At each level of awareness be aware of the inspiration and support you receive to help in your personal growth and encourage others to take this practice as well. As you go deeper and find that connection you'll find that each entity is unique in its own. As it tries to express it will eventually get powerful and creative enough to show itself to the physical world. More often then not it usually sends forth a message of wisdom, guidance and love.

Mediums try to accommodate those who ask but sometimes our friends and family members on the other side aren't ready to make that contact. Oh, they will when they feel it's the right time and when they know you're ready and more receptive of their spiritual blessing.

Meditating brings sensitivity and attunement to your energy along with a strong mental balance into your vibration. Think positively with love and accept yourself totally as who you really are so you can be free and fulfilled by this inner joy. Expect the unexpected and release any built up emotional blocks that you may have stored up. Listen to the subtle voice of your intuition, follow your impulses and act spontaneously. Your best tool is to see clearly a reflection of yourself with clarity and accuracy for a divine entity is the essence of a divine consciousness. When we discover the world of spirit it's like being reborn into the wonderful light of God.

I'll repeat myself here somewhat but it will relate a greater understanding. The two basic types of mediumship are mental and physical.

Mental mediumship involves the relating of information through communication via the varied aspects of thought transference or mental telepathy. Mental mediumship takes place within the consciousness of a medium. Mental telepathy is the relaying of information via thought without using any of the five physical senses. The results are expressed verbally and are passed through the medium's mouth. It's the medium that hears, sees and feels what the spirit communicators are relating. It is the medium's function to relate this information to the recipient of the message as they receive it under and through various states of control, such as clairvoyance, clairaudient, clairsentient and trance.

Physical mediumship involves the manipulation and transformation of physical systems and energies. The spirits are causing something to happen upon the earth plane. What happens varies with the style of mediumship involved but the results can be seen and heard by others such as visual, auditory, tangible, old factory and spiritual healing.

Clairvoyance is the power or faculty of discerning objects not present to the senses and the ability to perceive matters beyond the range of ordinary perception. This is subjective or objective; as with impressions subjectively the medium receives impressions that trigger a mental image; as in objectively the medium sees the spirit appearing in physical surroundings.

Psychometry is a form of clairvoyance, as in holding an object one gets impressions through touch that tell the story of the object or place.

Clairaudient is the power or faculty of hearing something not present to the ear but regarded as having objective reality perceived as voices and or words. Sometimes voices can be heard objectively although it's rare; this is considered indirect voice.

Clairsentient is feeling or the sensing of a spirit entity, which is the most common perception.

Trance is a state of partly or completely suspended animation or inability to function, a somnolent state as in reference to deep hypnosis and a state of profound abstraction or absorption as in the manifestation for the purpose of healing, speaking, writing and painting through spirit. Trance requires the medium to have the ability to disassociate them self from everyday consciousness to enter a state where spirit takes control, partially or complete. As the consciousness goes from light to deep it deepens or rises to a higher consciousness. As the consciousness withdrawals the spirit entity becomes more pronounced.

An evaluation of these expressions as in physical mediumship is: visual such as levitation, movement of objects, spirit lights, transfiguration, apports, table tipping, independent writings, spirit painting, photography, ectoplasmic hands, materialization, computer screen, (which had happened to a friend not of Spiritualism,) and television images, Auditory such as raps, music, direct and independent voice and electronic voice phenomena. Olfactory are spirit fragrances and other odours; tangible such as breezes and touches.

Some examples are: Visual as in levitation is the rising or lifting of a person or thing by means of the supernatural as in spirit assistance. Movement of objects as in a séance room or not, if the right medium is in the right place and the right frame of mind; this is done also through the supernatural and spirit helpers as in guides or a control. Spirit lights as in colors seen about a person such as an aura or flashes or colors associated with materializing of an entity. Transfiguration is a change in form or appearance and an exalting or spiritual change such as transfiguration of Christ on the mountaintop.

(I personally witnessed a spirit entity transfigure himself over a medium in trance. I knew this entity was for me from the way I felt. His full name was given and when I checked with my mother I was made aware that I knew this man when I was a small child but had forgotten about him.)

Auditory such as raps heard from Kate and Maggie Fox as of the beginning of Spiritualism; raps received and the code broken as a form of communication. Music, which is often heard in some meditations without music playing in the background, such as chimes. Direct, independent voice and electronic voice as in trance with a spirit using the mediums voice that is closer to their own other then the mediums. Independent voice as in a séance with the use of a trumpet; electronic voice as in receiving a call from a spirit friend via the telephone of a message left on your voicemail. Sometimes you may feel that you're being communicated via voice through the movement of certain and different objects and things in your environment. All things are possible when dealing with the spirit world.

Olfactory is related to or connected with the sense of smell as in spirit fragrances and other odours. Example, if a man was a farmer in his lifetime you may smell the farm aromas or the farm animals. If a person were a hairdresser you'd smell the scent of the salon/parlour, which is easily recognized.

Tangible is capable of being perceived especially by the sense of touch, as in substantially real and capable of being precisely identified or realized by the mind appraised at an actual or approximate value, such as breezes and touches from the entity/spirit that's making the connection with you.

Trance requires the medium to have the ability to disassociate them self from everyday consciousness to enter a state where spirit takes control, partially to complete. As the consciousness goes from light to deep it deepens and rises to a higher consciousness. As the consciousness withdrawals the spirit entity becomes more pronounced. The merits of trance, which means a reward or a punishment due, the qualities or actions which constitute the basis of one's deserts as in risking one's self for the process and a praiseworthy quality, as in an accomplished feat where spirit had been brought through and validated. The merits of trance, as in good, is the reward received when you have accomplish the connection and brought through a spirit from the astral for those still here on the earth plane, and of granting that individual a last chance to communicate with their beloved. This has to be one of the greatest gifts of all. Just knowing and watching the reactions of the sitter when proof had been given, such as an entity that has been called, finally comes through for those that need consolation and validation that their loved ones are still alive in spirit, and willing to make that contact, is phenomenal. The merits of trance, as in bad, are that one is never guaranteed what entity will take over when one is new and inexperienced. Once given control to a spirit a beginner should be in the company of an experienced medium to take charge if things happen to go wrong or sour. This is recommended for the wellbeing of the trance medium as deep trance mediumship is totally controlled by a guide/spirit/entity when they disassociate themselves and withdrawals completely. Harry Edwards, a great spiritual healer said, *"Trance is a mental control and not a physical possession."* Complete trance is complete control of the medium and she/he doesn't recall what had been said. A light trance is the opposite and one is usually aware of what had been said.

The historical source of trance has its lessons for the new and the old. We learn from our pioneers and from the ignorance of others that we Do Not abruptly touch a medium while in trance.

The New Age Movement is very different from Modem Spiritualism. New Age looks at transforming individuals and society through spiritual awareness. Its vision is an era of harmony and progress, comprising individuals such as activist groups, professional groups and spiritual leaders etc. They have brought the ecological, spiritual, and human-potential concerns into the mainstream in the 1980s, thus creating a large market in the United States and other countries for books, workshops etc., as well as for natural foods, crystals, meditation and healing aids. Their techniques for self-improvement, individual responsibility and self-healing have brought new creations to the world. This has found its way in health care; counselling, sports; the armed forces, and some corporations have provoked debate in religious and other circles. New Age thinking and practice has also influenced holistic attitudes about medicine, environment, family, work and most of all world peace. Ideas frequently associated with the New Age movement include anthropomorphic sophistic teachings, inner transformation, reincarnation, extraterrestrial life, biofeedback, chanting, alchemy, yoga, transpersonal psychology, shamanism, martial arts, the occult, astrology, psychic healing, extrasensory perception, divination, astral travel, acupuncture, massage, tarot, Zen, mythology, and visualization. New Age groups regard contact with the spirit world as channelling. Spiritualism in itself, as a religion, knows of channelling but prefers to call spirit contact spiritual communication as in trance. There is a big difference between channelling and an actual contact from a loved one. Spiritualism does not totally agree with the New Age Movement but has very similar beliefs.

Other religions of the world are quite similar with little differences that have included bits and pieces gathered from past sources and knowledge. For example some of the spiritualist followers tend to believe in reincarnation, where as some are dead set against it. I feel this is a personal choice, and we as individuals have this freedom of choice, so therefore some of the followers believe but keep it at a very low profile. When it comes to a personal belief follow your heart. What does it matter what the next person thinks when it's chosen with love for the betterment of yourself and others.

Chapter Two
Psychic Phenomena

A Prayer Recognizing God's Loving Power

Holy Spirit Divine:
You had guided me on a path of understanding your law
The powers that be are within my grasp
Protect and lead me on the path of righteousness
Wrap your loving arms around me as I envision the light of
passed loved ones
Bring our souls together as we commune between two
different worlds
Bind our love in your heavenly embrace
For eternity
Amen

Psychic relates to psyche. It means as found in Webster's dictionary, *lying outside the sphere of physical science or knowledge, immaterial, moral, and spiritual in origin or force. Sensitive to non-physical or supernatural forces and influences marked by extraordinary or mysterious sensitivity, perception, or understanding, and a person who is apparently sensitive to non-physical forces and psychic phenomena;* such as a Medium.

When you use your psyche you analyze; you anticipate and correctly identify your intentions and actions. So therefore we're all gifted with psychic ability and awareness. Some of us don't give this much thought; it's taken for granted as we go on with our daily lives. Others say they don't have this gift. They do, but it's buried deep within their subconscious mind. Psychic awareness is part of our natural endowment; a clairvoyant is psychic but a psychic is not necessarily clairvoyant, which is believed to be an accurate statement. It's time that people of the world finally become aware of the mysteries of their mind. We, all of us, have psychic ability, it's a gift beyond our five senses and we can learn to use it profitably. When we use it to help others and not for personal profit we'll learn more about ourselves. You need to look at your psychic ability as a means of personal growth and this tends to involve some sort of a radical transformation within yourself. Realizing your spiritual identity will intimately connect you at a spiritual level of awareness that can put you on a path of meaningful approach, of a self-concept.

Meditation on a daily basis opens up a new style of consciousness of psychic ability as well as brings on awareness from within your higher self, the God source.

Use this as a guide to tap into what God gave us all, psyche.

Dim lighting, quiet music and incense to bring about an inner peace, may be used. Focus on your breathing and await inspirational insight. Stay aware of your breathing without stopping the flow to quiet the mind and tune into your highest thoughts.

A sense of peace and being-at-one with life will connect you with the highest universal perspective. When you go within you come to accept whatever arises without any distress. Become one with it and penetrate the inner knowledge of your gifted psychic ability.

When you have a concern and would like answers go sit in a quiet place and meditate for a while. Open yourself up through meditation and allow focused points for an inner quietness of relaxation. This could include something such as a quiet flowing stream, visualizing yourself sitting in a beautiful field of wild—flowers or sitting by a light house looking out over a large body of calm water, just to name a few. A perfect scene to use is one that you're familiar with, such as a vacation spot that has left you with a beautiful memory. This gives you an idea of something that you may personally like to choose as your own focused point to bring awareness within your own vibration. Once your mind is clear of daily worries ask your question telepathically and wait on your higher self to give you an answer. Your inner self will resonate to a vibration giving you the correct awareness that is best for you in a given situation. Wait and see what manifestations of intuitive knowledge will come through for each question asked, based on your chosen focused point for relaxation. There may be some symbolic images and scenes that are often in a condensed pattern of information. You're the one that'll have to combine a creative answer and reveal it to your conscious mind. This ability acts as a vehicle from a source that is beyond your individual self and your ordinary reality. Once you've connected with an unseen universal force of information and insight use it for the brotherhood and the love of man. The more you use it the more powerful it will become. Don't be skeptical and critical, that will only create self-doubt.

Feel your energy as a basic vibration. It creativity arises at a spiritual level and then it enters a mental level of reality. The infinite extent of vibrations has implications for the communications that are involved. Psychic awareness, sensory consciousness and human imagination in conjunction with nature make mind and nature as one. This is where intuition and reality merge, coming together in a meaningful pattern. Like spirit contact, psychic awareness often involves perception through symbolism, leaving you to create the meaning. ESP on the other hand is a more direct form of perception.

All knowledge is within you and is guided by the highest form of reflection and activity. All you need to do is to seek it in a loving and creative way, which will be a positive reflection upon any given source.

The Hydesville rapping's was a revelation in itself as it was the beginning of the belief of an afterlife demonstrated in the public eye. It's the truth of spirit communication as the Fox family communicated with the so-called dead. The rapping's demonstrated survival of the material and rid a number of people from the fear of physical death of the body, therefore leaving the individual soul to continue existing and living on in the spirit world.

People needed proof and those that knew this were authentic and were about to give them just that. Some people believed that the dark rooms for the séances' concealed the practice of fraud. These people went on to become the first paranormal investigators of the era. While the Spiritualist movement brought the study of ghosts and spirits into the public eye it also provided fame for many of those involved. The mediums not only gain notoriety, so did many of the investigators and many experimental cases. Spiritualism wasn't meant to actually turn into a faith or a religious movement; it was a popular past time for many. The idea of communicating with the spirit world was an amusing way to spend a fantastic and enlightening evening, so to speak. There were a couple of factors that worked independently to cause Spiritualism to be inflated in importance and to be accepted as an actual religion. Despite the fact that many ministers of various faiths condemned it, the fact is that many accepted the possibility of strange events surrounding spirit communication and religious fervour at the same time.

Thanks to this evolution that lost loved ones were no longer lost. They could be communicated with and contacted as if they were still on the earth plane. This managed to fill a huge void for the everyday person who now had something to cling to and a belief that their friends and family-members had gone on to a better place. The raps were very important to mediumship development because something as wonderful as a continued life in spirit (after death) was the best news the world could have imagined to believe. This led to many years of research and many books have been written on the results which were very positive.

Here is an example of psych.

How often had you said, oh I shouldn't have gone? Or I should have listened to my gut feeling? And, I knew that was going to happen; or have a strong feeling of someone and then meet them on the street or in a shopping mall; or hear from them via telephone or email within a short time?

Let's look as if you were driving on a highway and something within you immediately says, '*stop for a coffee*'. You know that you don't really want one at this time but you feel that compulsion within so strongly. You get a sense of feeling that this is the right thing to do as for going ahead without it doesn't feel right. You listen to your psych and you pull off the highway and into the next coffee shop and do just that. This will probably take you about 10 minutes and then you're on your way again with a feeling of contentment. As you drive about half a mile you come upon and see an accident that had just occurred. You then realize that if you hadn't had such a feeling of uneasiness and hadn't stopped for that coffee you would have been right in the middle of it. Psychic intuition, guardian angels and spirit guides are with you continuously; listen and pay attention. Many don't listen but wished they had when something occurs, especially when they were given that intuitive insight and was made aware of by an uneasy feeling prior to its occurrence. Something of this nature happened to me; a crow came out of nowhere, flew down close to the highway in front of my car and I immediately thought of my father and heard him say, slow down son. My father was a man of few words so I listened and did as he said. That's right, there was an accident that occurred and I would have been in the middle of it if I didn't slow down. Intuition or is it protection from those that love us in the spirit world?

There's a Supreme Being behind all the diverse visible manifestations of the world. This Supreme Being we call God is within you as well as outside of you. Therefore, as you want to be loved and respected, love and respect others. Remember the golden rule and follow it to the best of your ability. Every living person and every living thing on earth is interconnected. You are a part of the whole creation. Your reality and your consciousness are out there as are all the people of the world. Realistically, from a universal or a space point of view, we're all out there as one unit.

There's a final dimension of the formula for psychic consciousness, which is mutual love. Love is the bridge that links you actively to the world. It joins you with the world in spirit, for the spirit of love is an essence of God.

Being psychic is being intuitive, following a gut feeling. We hear the word intuition many times during our lives. When you get a feeling that something isn't right, then it's not right for you. Follow your response of intuition and psychic awareness to your choices of decisions. Listen to your inner voice. That information is your psychic awareness. Trust in it, it's the God within you.

Chapter Three
God

A Prayer of Introduction to God

God, Divine Creator:
When I come to Your Garden I know I won't be alone
When I see the dew on the Roses I'll know of Your Divine
Presence
I'll hear your voice as you speak gently to me
The sound of your voice will be so sweet the birds will be
singing softly
I'll stay with you in Your Garden although the night is nearing
I'll feel you'll bid me to go walk and talk with you
I'll hear you tell me of the joy we'll share together
There's no other place I'd rather be but in your loving embrace.
Amen
(Created from a very well known song sung in various churches.)

How do you define God? What does the word 'God' mean to you?

We all have our own definition, whatever that may be; whether you live by traditional religious teachings or not, it doesn't matter as long as you follow your heart of the unconditional love of your fellow human counterparts, to the best of your ability. If you continue to always be aware of this you shouldn't go wrong. Just remember we're all divine and we're all from God whether we like our neighbour or not, they too are of God.

If you have a personal opinion of God, or have a certain religion, don't push it on anyone else, keep it to yourself. We're all entitled to our own opinions, whether it's God or any other given thing. If it were going to make another person or persons uncomfortable why would you want to cause this anguish and inflict a possible inner pain on your fellow man? Quite often this will cause another person to form an opinion of you and maybe you just won't like that opinion either. God don't judge you so why would you judge another's personal belief. In the Holy Bible in the book of Matthew, Chapter 5, verse 48 it says, *"Be ye therefore, even as your father which is in heaven is perfect."* If you're asked for an opinion that's different, then you'll have the permission of that individual. Step lightly on any given subject or topic you feel that is potential threats to another's opinion until you get a sense for any wanted or unwanted information. After all this belief is of a personal nature and should be respected. If you sense something the other person doesn't really want to hear, cut it short and gently change the subject. Most of us believe in the existence of the soul beyond death, so what does it matter in which way or through whom other people worship the God of their choice. Follow the guidelines of love, peace and harmony and in that sense you're not pressing anyone else to make choices to appease others.

God dwelleth in us, and his love is perfected in us; the Holy Bible in the book of 1st. John, Chapter 4, verse 12.

Never underestimate the power of God and never decry

another's beliefs, especially those with who you're not in complete accord, it's the same God as your own. There's but one in our universe, known by many different names. We hear people mention universal force and universal law. They're referring to the powerful force and the law of God with its ruling ability. Some people even consider this to be God. Respect and worship in a way that feels right for you without condemnation; this of course is a personal choice and should come through enlightenment of the senses. Discount minor differences and cultivate only that which will be good for all concerned.

All things on earth is very precious; let your journey toward that presence be seen as proof of your relationship with yourself, others and God. You'll make the right choice when you feel that universal force flowing through you.

Ye are the light of the world. The Holy Bible in the book of Matthew, Chapter 5, verse 14.

I was taught the Christian faith during my childhood. My mother taught me about the wonderful teachings of Jesus. His teachings were very important to her and still are. I'm one of eight and not one of us went astray from her wonderful caring heart. Although she attended various churches, which she introduced to me, she still follows in Jesus' footsteps. This gives her inner strength and a connection to God. She sees Jesus as her saviour, as in a sense that he spoke of divine guidance; if this brings her peace and comfort in any way then why would anyone consider this wrong? This gained leadership directs her choices in life. She understood and taught her children that we're all God's sons and daughters, precious souls such as Jesus and many other great masters.

There's a God-conscious inside of all our hearts. People are supposedly substantially the same but there's often an occasional hunger for spiritual truth. God, whom I call Infinite Spirit, is the first fundamental of our universe; when prayers are offered for spiritual guidance nobody is turned away. You may not get exactly as you asked or want, but you'll receive what you need for your own personal spiritual growth. Spiritual reality is perception and not proof as such; therefore we all stand in our own different place when it comes to being as one with God.

Webster's Dictionary defines God as; *the supreme or ultimate reality: The being perfect in power, wisdom, and goodness, the one worshiped as creator and ruler of the universe. The Incorporeal-Divine-Principle ruling over all as Eternal Spirit. Infinite Mind. A being or object believed to have more than natural attributes and powers and to require human worship. One controlling a particular aspect or part of reality. A person or thing of supreme value and a powerful ruler.*

I refer to the Christian Bible often as well as the Holy Koran; I read both. Religious teachings say that God wishes for us to have compassion and forgive over and over again. But that's very hard to do for some. They figure once is enough and most often that's what they get, if that. A divine intelligence is always near by, you're never alone. God never stops loving; He loves and forgives and won't ever give up on you. He'll love you even when you don't love yourself; reassure yourself of this divine love because we're loved in our aspiring as well as in our stumbling.

God's existence is a subject that has occupied schools of philosophy and theology for thousands of years. The atheist has always believed that there was no beginning. The idea is that matter has always existed in the form of either matter or energy; and all that has happened is that matter has been changed from one form to another, but it has always been. The Humanist

Manifesto says, *"Matter is self-existing and not created."* That is a concise statement of the atheist's belief. Scientists said in, 'A practical man's proof of God', *"The atheist's assertion that matter/energy is eternal is scientifically wrong. The biblical assertion that there was a beginning is scientifically correct."* Why worry over something you cannot change? Make your own assumption and feel what is right for you.

Theologians refer to God as Omniscience, which means He knows everything. God is eternal and not subjected to time, decay or corruption. He's Infinite, the most pure and often the simplest. The source of all things and the highest purpose of your life, He's perfection and unconditional love. You'll only realize this when you get to know him personally. If you like a better understanding, you'd learn a lot if you read about the teachings of Jesus. You're not looked down on because of the colour of your skin or being connected with a certain creed or your place of origin. He doesn't put one or the other on a pedestal. God sees only one race on earth and that's the one He created, 'the human race'.

Most mediumship demonstrations are usually God's messages. I say most because some are fraudulent and only there for material and personal gain. With false prophecy, and one totally believing in the message or reading, is subjected to manipulation. In so doing one is apt to fall for tricksters and lose a lot of money unwisely. Don't fall for this battering; believe in the fact that nothing or no one can harm you unphysical. There's no death of the soul and all who have passed-on still live; therefore those that love you will give only the best as love do not die beyond the grave; the spark of divinity continues to dwell within.

The Theo-Quest learning centre says. *"Your desire to learn more about God is evidence that you've already found him. The* desire to find God is proof that he has found you but you don't know him well enough to recognize him. The desire to know God is evidence that the true spirit of God lives within your heart. If more people knew about the goodness and the love of God then they could be led to live a new, deeper and richer life. All good things come to us from the Father of light, He does not change or shift, He's steady in his affection for all his children. We come to know God through our own personal experiences. God is beautiful, loving, merciful, positive and personal. Most importantly, He's your spiritual Father and you are his child. Begin a relationship with this marvellous God and begin your eternal life."

Albert Einstein said, *"Science without religion is lame; religion without science is blind."*

HOW many times have we heard or said, *"God help me or give me a sign that you exist?"* Often the reply is vague and ambiguous but maybe the phone rings or you hear an inner voice and think it's of your own mind. Something may fall from out of the blue, such as a book from a shelf that catches your attention. You may see something that reminds you of the past or something you hoped for in the future. We all want to know if God exists; recognize and appreciate any reliable method that comes to you to let you know that's He's with you.

God was worshiped but many followers; His Divine name from ancient times, as in certain faiths, is known as YHWH, or Yahweh, in Hebrew. From greater understanding YHWH has both male and female energies. From personal research the name was regarded as sacred; so sacred that it was ineffable and it was not to be pronounced so therefore *'Adonai, Lord or Elohim, God'* was used. This was widely accepted and practised throughout ancient history. In the Jewish tradition God's name is seldom ever mentioned but is often referred to as

'Hashem,' meaning, the Name. God has many names from various religions.

Dr. David Frawley said, *"As a universal formulation Hinduism accepts all formulations of Truth. According to the universal view there is only One Reality, but it cannot be limited to a particular name or form. Though Truth is one it is also universal, not an exclusive formulation. It is an inclusive, not an exclusive oneness—a spiritual reality of being— consciousness—bliss, which could be called God but which transcends all names. The different Gods and Goddesses of Hinduism represent various functions of this One Supreme Divinity and are not separate Gods. Without recognizing the feminine aspect of Divinity one cannot claim to know God. To recognize the feminine is necessary to restore wholeness, completeness and universality."*

We've all heard stories about the beginning of time and how it's referred to as what's said in the Bible in the book of Genesis. For many the first week of God's creation is of most importance and mentioned throughout history; it's preached about and discussed time and time again. The first chapter of Genesis tells about how God created each day of the week, which some say consisted of many hundreds of years, and how He rested on the seventh day. The first day consisted of the making of light and darkness, dividing it into day and night; earth wasn't first to be made.

The second day, Heaven was made; dividing the waters that existed within the void.

The third day earth 'appeared' and the creation of many grasses, herbs and trees were brought forth.

The forth day the sun and moon were created making day and night. Take notice that God made light and darkness in the first day but made the sun and moon on the forth, where did the light come from the first three days? It came from God, the Divine source; moreover, God is the source of all light. You have this ability, to sense, feel and witness this same light first hand through deep meditation.

The fifth day God created the living things in the waters as well as which crawl the earth and all that fly.

On the sixth day God wanted to create man. It appears that in the book of Genesis, Chapter one verse 26, that he didn't make this decision all on his very own, it says, *"And God said, let us make man in our image, after our likeness: and let them have dominion over...etc."* Then the following verse 27 says, *"So God created man in His own image."* Further on it tells how He did that. He created man from the dust of the ground and breathed in his nostrils the breath of life and man became a living 'soul'. Just look at that, if you believe the scriptures, right from the beginning we're informed that man is a living soul. Believe it and open your heart to a better understanding that you did come from a divine source.

Who was God referring to, who was he speaking with when he said, *Let us make man in our image after our likeness?* I'm not trying to be facetious here but whom was he addressing, a committee? Was he speaking to other Gods? Was he speaking to his God or his father? Who is he referring to as us? Who is our? Are there other Gods that govern other worlds? Do they all congregate together for comparison or group together to make suggestions and decisions to better their domain? The questions could go on and on.

Why is so much emphases based on the Bible? It was written by man, supposable received from a divine source. Who questions this but those who are able to receive spiritual contact them selves, knowing in their heart and soul that it's an interpretation of what was shown and telepathically received such as a medium with clairvoyant powers. Looked on today by specific beliefs as known in biblical times, as a Medium

Buddhism doesn't believe in a God. Judaism follows the Old Testament of the Bible as well as Christians. Islamic religion accepts Moses and Jesus and many others as prophets; they have their own bible-book as do many other organized religions. I've read scripture books of various religions and they all consist of harsh words directed at the human race. Sometimes I ask myself, why this and why that when God is so loving and merciful. Furthermore, the Mormons have a long tradition of carefully documenting death bed visions for over a hundred years. They've gotten a wonderful view of first hand knowledge of God and the afterlife.

What is the meaning of life? I often heard the saying, 'live and learn' and had said it a few times myself; each day we do learn something.

What is the meaning of death? We all have our own ideas on this. Such as knowledge taken from others teachings and knowledge that we found stored in the depth of our own memory banks. As I had often heard in my spiritual travels from various people publicly speaking *"there's no such thing as death."*

That I truly believe. The Bible in the book of Matthew, Chapter 5, verse 14 it says, *"Ye are the light of the world."*

Sometimes I like a non-Spiritualism friend's point of view, on certain things. I asked one of them on how he sees God and what part God plays in his life, and his beliefs in the afterlife. This is what he said. *"That's a tough question but God has always been around me in my life. In my upbringing, Sunday school, plus Sunday church service. Seeing my mom my grandma with their bibles, my aunt watching her Evangelists TV shows to seeing my Muslim friend praying 5 times a day, every day. Then it's how I personally see God. It's been a personal quest all my life in trying to figure God out. Mostly when I feel vulnerable and don't know what's happening to me or where I'm heading, I talk to him. When I'm scared, I pray. Sometimes, when things are good, I thank him. I see him as an entity that I can't visualise. I see death as entering a state of knowing everything, things we can't fathom here while alive. I believe it all could become clear than, and then I have my doubts as my scientific schooling feeds that. Sometimes I'm down about the possibility of death being the end and then I say, but it makes no sense. I could go on at length but it comes straight from the heart for that's just the eternal quest for finding out what it's all about."*

Everything in life has a purpose. Satan is the evil force, which also plays a role in our lives, for without the bad we wouldn't have such a great respect for the good.

Sri Yukteswar says, *"It's the Spirit of God that actively sustains every Form and Force in the universe; yet He is transcendental and aloof in the blissful uncreated void beyond the worlds of vibrations."*

Jesus, Krishna, St. John, Gandhi, Pantanjali, St. Paul, Kabir, Mohammed and other prophets are all past Masters. A lot of us have learned a great deal by recognizing that the loving messages received and the teachings of unconditional love are of a divine source.

An infinite intelligence pervades and controls the universe. It's without shape or form; it's impersonal, omnipresent and omnipotent, which is God—the light giver. The Light of God removes darkness immediately; we're very fortunate to be in that all pervading everlasting light whether it's at night or during the day; light (knowledge, spiritual awareness and insight) is with you always. You need only to accept this as fact and recognize that it's there; you often accomplish this through meditation.

I asked another friend about God. He said, *"God is our creator and we have to respect him in our own way; He gave us life. The Bible says God created us in his own likeness, to love and to respect each other. Sometimes I think what a troubled world we're in when I see the harsh crimes, devastation and destructions on earth then there are people in the likeness of God."* Unfortunately, at times this appears to be gaining the upper hand but look at all the love from humanity when disaster or devastation strikes or takes place through natural law; billions of people are there to assist with unconditional love.

I was drawn to a little book that was thrown amongst others things on a table at a yard sale. One word on the cover caught my eye. The title is, *'I was afraid I'd lose my soul to a chocolate malt'*, written by Mike Tighe. The word soul stood out and I picked it up. He states in this little book that the perfect prayer is the Lords Prayer. He must have done some research because he goes on to say that Jesus Christ did not compose it. Further on he says, *"Does it matter who composed the Our Father when what is more important is living its message?"*

To accomplish a high quality mediumship through psychic awareness you need to open your heart and meet God in your daily life. God is perfect and all-powerful; He is Spirit. One need not picture God as a once human being; this imposes limitations, He's not of a human spirit. He's the creative universal Spirit. Wherever there is life, there is Spirit; and wherever there is spirit there is life. We exist because a spark of divinity is within us; this divine relationship, (in which God is recognized as Father and or Mother or both), confirms that we are all the creator's children.

You have freewill to reject and ignore that which you feel is of value or not in your life. Sometimes you'll fail to progress, as you should, by denying yourself what life has to offer. Be alert and try always to make wise decisions. Who will hurt the most by deciding unwisely?

When our great prophets and messenger's eons ago started to write words of wisdom, love, harmony, peace and words to make you fear a God who loves you, they had the idea and hopes of creating subtlety. When one has a desire to be humble, prosperity will succeed and remember, discretion will preserve you as it probably had many times during your lifetime.

A dear friend of mine is a 74 year old woman. She was raised a Roman Catholic and remains devoted to her religion. Although she had a very strict religious background she remains open to other people's views and has a sister that's a Medium. She presented me with a poem she received from her church. The words flowed in rhythm and were very nice. The message was that if you carried a cross in your pocket or on you God would protect you. If you feel protected by carrying a small cross on your person then by all means do so. I was also raised with a somewhat belief.

Once I got home I sat and meditated on what I had read and then I began to write. Below is my answer to her poem. I gave her a copy to place along side of the one she has. She accepted it and appreciated my interest.

A Reminder of God

You carry a cross in your pocket a Christian you may be
It's not magic, a good luck charm or a means to protect thee
That cross is a reminder of a price he had to pay
But for what reason had he died on that frightful day
You strive to serve him better in everything you do

But God protects from physical harm and takes care of you
The cross simply reminds us to comfort and bring peace
Yet Jesus is our brother and that will never cease
He'll be there when you need him as well as God above
A Christian will go through him reaching for divine love
For God our infinite spirit is the one and only law
No need to have a reminder he will not let you fall
Jesus Christ is Lord to a person of Christian faith
But as a renowned Spiritualist living by God's grace
Infinite Spirit my master, Jesus Christ my brother
Divine Spirit and Jesus Christ I love you like no other
Connecting God through another source doesn't do any harm
Allah, Buddha, Mother Mary welcomes with open arms
We're all connected to our God and if it satisfies you
Continue on with what you do but respect the other few
That directly goes to the greatest source Infinite Spirit Divine
I do this with my daily prayer, cause a true God as this is mine.

God don't test you.
Maybe it's just natural law that's at work.
Sometimes it's what we bring on ourselves.
But, once gotten past the hurt, one is always aware of what was learnt and often benefits from the teachings.
In my youth I questioned different religions and their recognition of God. With a greater spiritual awareness I found what I felt deep within during my lifetime. I found the lost part of my soul's existence and am very pleased with my decisions regarding religion. Some of it is based on my mother's guidance, which is from God through Jesus, so who's to say her choice is wrong. You too have this God spark, the spark of the Divine, known as Light. If you read books about life after death based on out-of-body experience you'll come to a conclusion

that many experiences deal with being somewhat in a tunnel with light at the end, which they feel is from God. Those experiences happen after the heart stops beating declaring physical death.

Once you realize God's laws, Natural Laws, are unchanging you'll begin to accept your neighbour's decision on life matters involving moral ethics and a god of choice. Once you feel that peace within, both neighbours will live in harmony side by side, as we're all connected through an unseen source.

God's not an old man sitting on a throne in heaven. He's all around and inside of every living soul on this planet. While God is watching over us all at once we're all connected by this holy energy source.

Imagine the earth as a baseball. Then imagine a camera focused entirely over all the people of the earth. This camera eye, who I'll call God, is sending beams or rays of light in billions of directions directed to every continent, every state, every country and every town, right down to the individual person. This, if given thought, would look something like a disco light in a night club and I assume the majority has seen such a light. Therefore, all Souls are inner connected by the Great Divine Spirit. We may not be connected directly to one another but this wonderful Infinite Spirit, we call God, connects us indirectly.

A person can be persuaded in choosing almost anything but as long as you feel that divine inner connection then who can honestly say that you made the wrong choice? We all have the capacity of belief to guide one to successful actions in making a decision when we seek guidance from another. Take into consideration, all things must be understood as aspects of an absolute totality. We have to be personally responsible for decision making and be accountable for our actions. The only reality is mind, yours, everyone's and mine. Anything less than reality itself is self-contradictory and contradiction usually predicates.

We as humans of the finite self expand into the absolute self through religion, science and being loyal to a wider community creating a spontaneous energy of the evolutionary process. Each of us will then have a feel for intuition as opposed to nature of science, and science minded philosophy. The British philosopher Alfred North Whithead says, *"Things are not unchanging substances having definite spatial boundaries, but are living processes of experiences embodying eternal objects, or universals, fused with them by God."*

The 19th-century romantic revolt of existential philosophy became influential in Germany by Martin Heidegger. He stresses on intense emotional experiences with conception of negation as a real force. His philosophy substitutes Nothingness for God as the source of human values. His friend Jaspers finds God as Transcendence in the intense emotional experiences of human beings. Jose Ortega y Gasset of Spain defended intuition against logic and criticized the mass culture and mechanized society of modern times. Austrian-born Zionist author and scholar Martin Buber, combining Jewish mysticism with strains of existential thought interpreted human experiences as a dialogue between the individual and God.

Beloved, let us love one another: for love is God; and every one that loveth is born of God. The Holy Bible, 1st. John, Chapter 4, verse 4.

What do you think about the power of God? How many have prayed and got their prayers answered? How many have prayed and felt their prayers have gone unheard and then felt an anger towards God? Many people doubt and many have wandered away from any belief whatsoever. Who do you turn to when there's a crisis way beyond your capabilities and understanding? Give it some thought. It doesn't matter how often you go to church; God does not expect you to go there every chance you get, you can connect to the source at home. Sure, it's nice to go to an environment where you hear the silence and feel the energy source all around you. You can get that same feeling sitting right at home in your own living room. God will not judge you and He loves you way beyond your comprehension. Sit quietly at times, close your eyes in silence and see what God has to say to you. Be open and receptive to anything you hear and you'll know when God has made contact. Intense prayer is one way of doing this, followed by meditation in your own comfortable quietness and safe surrounding.

I have prayed many times throughout my life. Some prayers got answered quickly, some took a little longer and some went unanswered because they weren't meant to be. The universal law of God could not change what was inevitable and way beyond my reach. An unchanging force uncomprehendable often paves destiny's way.

A personal example: I have an incurable illness, known as Bi-Lateral Meniers Disease, it's an inner ear problem that involves the deterioration of the nerves resulting in vertigo, dizziness and hearing loss. It doesn't permit me to continue with my personal life as to be able to continue in the work field; who ever thought this would happen to me; very familiar words right?

I have permission to share this story with you as it involves someone else.

I have two Chihuahuas, male and female. The first litter of puppies about a year ago were three black and one 'black and tan', making a total of four. Three were like the mother and one like the father. The black and tan puppy went out of the province to a friends' neighbour. He took this little puppy everywhere; no matter where he went the puppy went along.

While driving his wife to the city to see her specialist and two hours on the highway they were involved in a head-on collision, a major car accident; both cars demolished and written off. His wife died instantly as well as the little six-month-old puppy. This man barely hung on to life and was hospitalized in critical condition for about three months. While in a coma in an Intensive care unit I told my friend to whisper in his ear that if he lives he'd get a replacement puppy. He slowly progressed and was eventually discharged from the hospital. He was very anxious to get another puppy to help ease his loss and emotional pain. The loss of his wife and his little puppy friend was very difficult to cope with emotionally. Upon his discharge he phoned and I had good news for him that his new puppy was on the way: (Please note I did not and do not breed dogs for material gain other then a companion to someone that's in need.)

My little female Chihuahua loved her tummy rubbed when she was pregnant. About two weeks before the delivery date I was rubbing her tummy. As a child I always wanted a pure white Chihuahua; I closed my eyes, with my hand on her tummy, I spoke out loud to God. I prayed very intensely with a feeling of connecting with God, Infinite Spirit. I said, *"Dear God, I know you have the power and the ability to do anything you wish to do. I know I'm going to ask for a lot, but may I please have a little white puppy and another black and tan male for my friend. Amen."*

Two weeks later on a day off I noticed the little mother-to-be in labour. I took her, wrapped her in a blanket and sat with her in my arms in the sunroom. I gently rubbed her tummy as I often did; it seemed to help ease her pain and gave her comfort. I was speaking quietly to her while she shifted with each contraction. Then suddenly I felt her pushing a little longer than previously and knew something happened. I lifted the sheet to take a look and right before my eyes was a little pure white puppy. Elation beyond excitement doesn't describe my feelings. I felt such a strong divine connection as all life is precious. I broke the sack from her little nose so she could breathe on her own and then I jumped up with joy. While holding the mom and the baby I shouted out, *"Thank you God, Thank you God, Thank you so much for answering my prayer. Thank you for my little white puppy."*

I took them both to their room downstairs. I assisted in the delivery and cut the cord as the little mother doesn't like to have anything to do with her puppies until all are born. Lo and behold the next puppy was the replacement for the one that died in the accident; it was a male with the exact markings. There were three more born, one was very tiny 'white and cream female' that died two hours after birth due to breathing problems. The next was 'white and tan' and the last one was 'white and black'. I loved them all.

Once again, the little mother weighing about six pounds is totally black with a little white under her chin and the sire dog is black and tan. God answered my prayers, gave me what I asked for and gave me a bonus of two other unusually beautiful puppies. Thank you God for your wonderful gifts.

The puppies were four weeks old and my white puppy was the only one that didn't have a name. I tried to come up with something that was ideal for her, but Sugar or Ivory just didn't seem to fit. I heard a voice inside of me saying, *"It will come to you in time."* I let it go. (Always listen to this inner voice) When they were about 5 weeks old I went down to their room. I sat on the floor and all four of them crawled in my lap. As they did I picked them up and called them by name. When it came to my little white puppy, the last one to be able to succeed the struggle of climbing, I said, *"Your God's little gift to me."* Then a flash of thought entered my mind, I spoke again and said, *"You're God's Gift; your name will be G.G."* She finally got her name.

Chapter Four
Reincarnation

An Affirmation of Rebirth

Great creator of all:
You've granted me another lifetime in a material world.
Lessons learned will take me to a higher level of your divine love
There were difficult times but the good remains close to my heart
I've chosen my life with the guidance of you
As you watch over and protect me I feel your reassurance of
my progression
My will is of acceptance to its destiny As I lay asleep each
night my soul will soar towards its future home
There's a new beginning when this life ends amongst its
fellow souls
I'll be greeted with love, I'll live in peace until I rebirth.
Amen

Reincarnation means, as according to Webster's dictionary, *the action of reincarnating, the state of being reincarnated, rebirth in new bodies or forms of life and a rebirth of a soul in a new human body.*

Some people don't believe in reincarnation and that's their

personal choice; therefore one shouldn't be forced to think otherwise. A personal belief, as which the God you choose differs from others, likewise should a belief in rebirth. Help reduce ignorance and assist with the repair of damage created by such unknown awareness.

Developing and refining your mind is probably the most important thing you can do as a spiritual individual or human being. I feel that when we die our souls separate from our bodies and take on a whole new existence and form into another life.

Just recently I was walking on the street and saw a poster with a young man sitting down and the words saying, *"I don't remember hitting the ground."* This was an advertisement for an insurance company. I felt a stillness come over me as I read the words, and heard telepathy, *"That's right, he wouldn't remember, feel or be aware of hitting the ground because his soul left the body just prior to the impact."* The mind is connected with the activity of the brain, totally separate from the soul. Our awakened soul, fully opened to conscious development is characterized by a state of perpetual peace. The Pineal gland, the small conical appendage of the brain is connected directly with the third eye and is in relation with the subconscious mind, descending down the spinal column. It's also considered the seat of the soul. I was told by a very experienced medium, who will be identified in a short while, that the soul lies within the solar plexus around chakra number three; being that when you follow your gut feelings you're following your soul's awareness. An avid meditator would probably have had experienced this already.

In Tibet, the Tulkus or Rinpoches are individuals who when nearing death will sit up if they have the power to do so and go into a meditative state so that their souls will pass though the veil, finally breaking free the chains of reality. Those that are in the environment of the dieing don't interfere with this traditional method of death, they do what they feel deep in their heart is the right thing. In addition, they are encouraged and assisted if needed. When the soul leaves the body it finds itself floating upward to other levels and is often met by loved ones and family members. They're onward bound as the soul travels to its newer existence and the next experience that awaits them on the other side. There's always hope of a possible coming back, reincarnated into another body, for those that believe. These very religious individuals are known as the Precious ones of Tibet. Tibetan people have a deep compassion for peace, harmony and love for all people of the world and this is where their loyalty rests.

One way to understand yours and everybody else's nature is through love and kindness expressed from the very heart of your soul. An enlightened energy is a prayer for the world, given daily by each and every one of us. When we want peace in the world we need to have tolerance for our neighbour, our fellow man and all people regardless of race, creed or colour. Make your choice in religion with compassion, along with your chosen God. As long as it's coming from your heart with love, you're on the right track.

The gateway to peace is very narrow and the only way to enter it is through your own soul. Once your soul has left its captive embodiment it has an option of staying on the earth plane or it may go to other planes as it desires when that part of its development had met its criteria.

According to Buddha we have lived many unaccountable lifetimes of every life form since the beginning of time. Give this some thought and imagine yourself living in the days of Jesus Christ and what you would have possibly been doing at that time.

To distinguish between reincarnation and rebirth it's understood that in rebirth we have no choice of the soul's destiny; it's a new creation by God and God has chosen the path and the lessons to be learned, making it involuntary.

In reincarnation it's understood that the soul has free will of being in control of its impulses and involuntary actions, giving it the ability to be able to choose its next destination prior to rebirth.

With extra thought given, we must not confuse the mind with the brain because the seat of the mind lies within the heart. The brain can be used for self to conquer self, given the right format of enlightenment. Also take note that when it comes to reincarnation karma plays a major role, 'what we sow shall we reap'. Meaning, what you've done to others so shall it happen to you in the next life, if you hadn't experience something similar in this lifetime. Don't continue the same pattern, learn to love and accept, making your next reincarnation more pleasant without karmic attachments from past lives.

I met a young man when I was at the age of 25 and we became very good friends that lasted until his death. Unfortunately his earth existence ended when he was only 43. I collect coins and banknotes as a hobby from all over the world since the age of 18. When people know you have an interest like this they'll contribute if the opportunity arises. Most people who want to give gifts on certain and special occasions don't have a problem of knowing what to give me. They never go wrong with an addition to my collection.

My friend contributed to this collection for years. When he travelled he brought back coins, as other friends did. When a special occasion came up, he'd give coins or banknotes whether foreign or domestic, sometimes in mint condition. I'm always grateful and very pleased with any contribution from anyone so willing to give. There's a particular incident that continues to remain in my consciousness. One day he phoned and said, *"I have a container of coins I found on the side of the road and you're welcome to come by to pick them up."* I went to his place a few days later; he went in a room adjacent the living room and brought the container out and placed it in my hands. When I lifted the cover to take a look, there was also a shiny gold ring on top which was amongst the coins when he found them. I hesitantly picked it up as soon as I saw it. He said it's also mine if I wanted it; (he had a chronic long-term illness and at this point in his short life he knew it was soon coming to an end.) I examined the ring and noticed it was 24K gold. The gold was very soft and the ring had taken on a slight oval shape, probably from being pressed together by something while it was being worn. There's a first name initial and a last full name engraved on the inside, surrounded by leaves. I put the ring on my finger and it fitted perfectly. When it was totally on I felt its comfort and had one of the most amazing visions I can remember. I immediately saw a tall thin man in his sixties of India descent. He looked at me and smiled as if he knew who I was. At that very moment I felt I was looking at myself from a previous life. I got a telepathic message saying you finally got back your long lost possession. Then he left as quickly as he came. I got a little emotional and didn't know what to say and confined my feelings. I took the ring off and proceeded to take a look at all the coins. 98% of them were from Sri Lanka. This verified the tall man I envisioned. I didn't say anything about my vision although my friend was well aware of an existence beyond our material world from experiencing several in his un-well state. I thanked him for his generous gift although it's not a special occasion and he said, *"All our occasions together as friends are special."* My friend passed to spirit a few months later.

I've always had a special place in my heart and felt very comfortable around people from India. I feel a special attraction of kindness towards Sri Lankan descents for some unknown reason, but it's for all of India in general.

A couple of weeks ago in my closed circle meeting, a young medium said, *"I see you in a past life. You're sitting down blowing a horn and there's a snake in front of you. I feel that you have a strong connection with India."* I didn't say anything to her at the time other than that I could relate to it. This, in a sense, could be a verification of a possible reincarnation for me as I felt with the ring. I wore this particular ring for quite some time; I was fascinated with the feelings related to it. When I saw this young medium again she held this ring to see if she could pick up any vibrations; as psychometry is a detection of energy passed from a held object to a person, such as that of a medium. Webster's dictionary says *it's a divination of facts concerning an object or its owner through contact with or proximity to the object.* She said that she got such a very strong feeling of love and compassion and became somewhat emotional. She immediately gave it back saying, *"This is a gift, cherish it."*

Past life memories can affect the quality of life we experience today in a more radical way. Although we may give considerable thought of this situation we can truly say that suffering, in one form or another, marks our lives during birth and death. We can go anywhere in psychic space but our multi-dimensional reality is actually achieved through our subconscious. Jesus said in Matthew, Chapter 12, verse 32. *"Neither in this world, neither in the world to come."*

The Hasidic Jews strongly believe in reincarnation. They believe that they themselves are the cause of their own situations and no one else was involved. I also feel we have a choice in what goes on with us on the earth plane prior to birth. The essence of the human being in reincarnation is that every opportunity for spiritual growth is precious at each lifetime. Then again in the Bible, in Ecclesiastes, Chapter 12, verse 7. It says, *the spirit shall return unto God who gave it.*

Although I'm not promoting Spiritualism or any other religion but Spiritualism and the Hasidic Jews have one thing in common. They don't bow to anyone but go directly to God. Spiritualist believers with their spiritual energies bow their heads in silence in a meditative state for the soul contact with God, the Great Divine; going deep within to a distant level of consciousness makes such a contact.

Knowledge is important to make your lives happier but the ancient laws of karma say you basically bring everything on yourself. Spiritual involvement, I feel, is the purpose of life on earth and our destiny cannot be changed, but we have the ability to make it easier or harder in our own environment and every day lives. We have to be accountable and take responsibility for ourselves and sometimes it's the personality that learns the lessons. Karma is not punishment but lessons learnt from cause and effect.

I was informed about a lady in Whitby, Ontario, Canada and was encouraged to invite her to read this book, my manuscript. It took sometime for me to get it together for presentation but within this time frame the universe seemed to have taken matters in hand. When I did finally get in touch and spoke of my request she told me that she had already discussed it with my contact and that she would be more then pleased to read it. This she did very willingly, with guided knowledge and information that she felt it needed. She agreed with the totality of it but said that she'd like to do a regression on me to show me all about past lives and reincarnation. She made time in her busy work schedule and gave me first hand experience with a mild form of hypnosis leading to past life regressions. I was a little anxious to give this a try but had a deep compulsion to have an experience. This advanced my knowledge with the development and learning of possibly living a previous lifetime. I say possibly as I have a great imagination but it sure felt as if I was reliving episodes of previous existences'.

The day finally came and I'm on my way to her house, a little nervous but very anxious and willing to be regressed, from my understanding, by such a well-experienced and capable medium. I arrived and was directed towards a reclining chair; I made myself comfortable and asked God for protection with a short prayer.

I sensed a well-adjusted and confident woman as she began to speak softly as I went into a meditative state. Once I was deep within, regression began.

I was taken back through my present life by ten years at a time until I reached the day I was born. From there I was taken to the spirit realm.

Once I was regressed that far I immediately saw myself in Baghdad as a salesman in a market selling jewellery. I wasn't there all that long because she directed me through a garden where the pathway was lined with crystals. As I kept walking through the garden and as I proceeded forward, the crystals were considerably larger in comparison. Eventually I came to the last one on my right, which was very tall and narrow with a well-defined pointed top. I was told to wrap my arms around it, which I did, and then was told to become one with it. I felt myself enter inside and now as I've melted into it I'm now looking out, through the crystal, at the outside. I'm in total command of the whole unit as I'm now the navigator. I was told to look upwards towards the tunnel and see the light at the end, and this I saw with clarity. I was told to go directly there with the crystal as my means of transportation. I was glad it had a pointed top so it would travel faster, much like a rocket. Deeper and deeper I went until I was told to exit at the other end; upon my exit I was brought to another previous lifetime.

I saw myself as a Muslim Arab man in the desert of Saudi Arabia, born of wealth and wisdom. I was one of several peacemakers who were in the desert to discuss peace and try to prevent a war from happening with another country. I was totally aware of my surroundings and could feel the heat and the hot sand beneath my feet. I was asked if there was anyone in my surroundings that's now with me in this lifetime and there wasn't. I was asked if I had a name and my name was *"Hamondi."* I was then taken outside of my body and told to hover above it and look at what was happening. I saw the peacekeepers' group, including myself, being slaughtered like animals in the wild by some of their own kind who wanted the war to go ahead no matter what the consequences. A sword was driven through my head entering through my right ear, which killed me.

I was then regressed to another previous lifetime.

I saw myself around the pyramids in Egypt. I was a slave woman who was badly treated by a few of the many men working on and building the pyramids. There were, from appearances, hybrid-aliens with humans that were in control of other humans; those hybrids were chosen to build the pyramids with the help of the people chosen from the human race. The aliens controlled everything from above but at a close range. I don't remember seeing them but I felt that they were looked upon as part of the Gods and that they were sent by God to do what they had to do. I felt very scared of all the action although most people were actually very good to me. There were human men who would use and abuse me because more than personal caring and cooking was required. I was asked if there was anyone there that's now in this lifetime with me and there wasn't. I was asked to leave my body and hover above to see what was happening. A man came towards me and started to physically abuse me. I didn't like this man and feared him. He was not someone I had a lot of contact with or saw regularly. He beat and raped me and finally killed me by continuous blows about the head with his fists. I wasn't the only woman there but my torture and slaying didn't seem to be noticed by anyone. I felt women were used more than loved and that little attention was given to them. I was not asked my name so I don't recall one.

I was then regressed to another lifetime and saw myself as a Monk in a cave in the mountains of Tibet. I was told to leave my body and hover above it; as I did I saw two people at the entrance calling my name. I felt safe as I knew who it was and went outside to greet them. They immediately grabbed me and held me down. They didn't think being in silence was important and were going to make it become a definite reality. They had something like metal rods in their hands, which were very hot and the smell of burning iron was evident. Both men drove one in each of my ears, laughing while doing so and ignoring my screams and struggles. I remember speaking out loud to my regressor saying, *"I don't like what I see and what's happening to me."* I was comforted and then I was asked if there was anyone in that lifetime that's now with me in the present one, and there was. Today this person is a very special friend that cares deeply for me and has been exceptionally generous for years; I prefer not to reveal the identity.

I was then commanded to go back through the tunnel and back to my present existence. Then Rev. Dr. Alva Folkes brought me gently back to reality.

Due to such an emotional experience from my life as a monk my eyes were a little damp from the trauma I witnessed. I came back to my senses and thought about what just occurred; I was very pleased with having one of the best experiences of my life, although I saw myself suffer in three of them. I can now relate to my illness if one carries past-life idiosyncrasies.

Reverend Dr. Alva Folkes states that each reincarnation works on different aspects of the soul and that we're never back identical.

Whether you believe or not, let other people freely express their views and also express yours. If two people disagree let it go and strive towards a friendship instead of your differences.

Chapter Five
Aura and Chakras

A Prayer, an Affirmation

God, our creator.
Within your eyes we're all brothers and sisters
Grant us wisdom to love one another
Make each step towards a personal goal
Guide each moment so we may live in harmony
Great Spirit, make peace on Mother Earth
Peace eternity.
Amen

(With inspiration from a hymn)

Aura, according to Webster's dictionary means: *a subtle sensory stimulus, a distinctive atmosphere surrounding a given source, a luminous radiation, and an energy field that is held to emanate from a living being.*

We all have an aura that can consist of all the colours of the rainbow. Some are much bigger then others. It depends on your environment, health, emotions and personal well being.

Mediums with clairvoyant powers are able to see them with the naked eye and give character readings just by looking at it. Good spiritual healers are often able to locate a disease from this particular luminous cloud that surrounds the whole body. Your aura is an emitted bodily energy that's of an invisible field totally surrounding you, consisting of several layers.

Ever notice when certain people move close to you and you feel a little uncomfortable? They're within your aura's energy field and more often then not you get a negative feeling from their aura when you experience such as this. Take notice of your actions the next time this happens, you'll automatically move away or step back to rid yourself of this feeling. Sometimes you may even put your hand up to stop them from coming any closer because the energy is to strong and you don't like the feeling from their aura energy field; and rightly so. Then at other times you may move closer, and you may even want them to move closer still because of the positive vibes you're receiving. This wonderful feeling of love and peace emitting from their aura to yours is often felt and thought of as an inner feeling not related to the aura. Those are the people who are on the same wavelength as your self. You may remember being in someone's company and wanting to hold them because you feel a sense of them needing a hug or a warm heart to comfort them in some way or another. People like this should be made aware of and feel that you are reachable for their comfort and understanding, to a certain degree.

Luminosity painting around the heads and full body, such as the halo, of important personages had been done for several years in ancient times. Romans, Egyptians and ancient Greek painters presented this in fashion around such important individuals.

Your aura will vary in size and colour. When you're happy,

well and healthy your aura is at its peak. This is the largest aura of all unless you're angelic and from a different realm of existence.

When a bond has been made between you, the medium, and the Spirit World the colour of the aura is quite phenomenal. There's direct spiritual contact and it glows with radiance. After all, the atoms of which we are made came from the stars, so it has been said. You and your soul are immortal and anything from God would have a radiant glow about them. It's the nature and inner workings of the human spirit shining through as there is some higher intelligence within guided by the natural flow of the divine. God evolves through human consciousness and the aura is very much a part of you; besides, you're created in His image.

When you feel sick or emotionally drained people will notice this and little do they know they picked this up from seeing a slight change in your personal aura. Your personal surrounding of a luminous cloud has changed and is very different from when they saw you last. Your distinctive aura will also change as you get older, and it differs with both sexes.

There are many things in the world to see that's invisible to the naked eye; things that you don't pay any attention to at first glance. Auras are very real. They have been photographed in laboratories; they're not illusions. When I look at an aura I look at a person as if I were looking at a 3D picture. You too will be able to see them with practise. This works for me but may not for you. Another way is to 'squint' your eyes or if you prefer half-close them and look intently at your subject from different angles and distances until you get the hang of it. You may also start by having someone stand in front of a wall or some other solid background. A white background with dim lighting works best for a beginner. Begin by looking at the wall behind your friend or partner; refocus your eyes as if you were looking at near and far distances', that's if you're able to do that. Look at the wall behind them but keep them in your vision as you look past them. You'll see a shade surrounding the head, that's the aura. Keep in mind that seeing an aura starts with you believing that you're able to; it will take time so don't give up on yourself.

The first aura that you see will probably look like a greyness about the head about an inch or so wide. The more you practice the better it stands out. Don't do this for long periods of time at the beginning; give yourself a set time so that you won't get a stinging or burning sensation in your eyes or end up with a headache.

The aura consists of the colours of the rainbow and so do your chakras. They both interact and work in unison when put to the task. Once you become aware of your aura and know how to put your chakras to use, in a spiritual and positive way, you're aura will be more pronounced, even to an individual who can't actually see it but can sense it.

Your chakra colours are the colours that are projected through your aura. Once one of your chakras is off balance it will show through your aura. They interact and portray dullness when you're ill as well as brightness when you're feeling exceptionally well. This projection of well-being is mentally as well as physically.

Chakra: (chä-kr) according to Webster's dictionary, *is any one of several points of physical or spiritual energy in the human body, according to yoga philosophy. Sanskrit chakra, literally wheel: a circular diagram of spectrum used to show the relationship between the colours.*

Chakras consist of seven major different coloured wheels, referred to as spiritual points by some. Your whole body is covered with chakras; some very small in size as well as those that are much bigger. Once chakras are opened you can use them as a single energy focus point or use them in totality, working together. When opened and put to use your psychic forces and bodily functions can merge and interact. The three main Chakras are: Number 7: Crown, top of your head. Number 4: Heart, centre chest and number 1: Base, end of the spine, but they all hold significance to each other and to your aura.

Diagram:

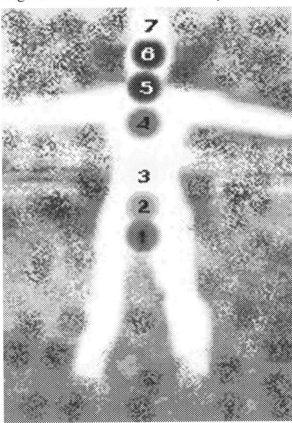

Beginners and student mediums are recommended not to open their Chakras before acquiring more knowledge about them and their actions. Search out a book on the subject or join a group where it's taught in the program. Shirley McClain wrote a book called, 'Going Within' and also made a VHS tape concerning the chakras. This tape is an excellent lesson if you're lucky enough to find it.

Number one is the Base, end of the spine. This is your grounding point. This one deals in relation with your fear, restlessness, prosperity, trust, health and physical dimension. Its colour is red.

Number two is the Sacral, over the genitals. This one deals in relation with your sexuality, emotions, desire, pleasure and creativity. Its colour is orange.

Number three is the Solar Plexus, over your abdomen. This one deals in relation with willpower, strength, self-esteem, vitality, sensitivity and personal power. Its colour is yellow.

Number four is the Heart, over your centre chest. This one deals in relation with self-acceptance, compassion, balance, relationships and love. Its colour is green.

Number five is the Throat, over your larynx. This one deals in relation with communication, expression, creativity, resonance, judgement and speech. Its colour is blue.

Number six is the Brow, centre forehead, directly between your eyebrows and connected with the pineal gland; it's considered your third eye. This one deals in relation with your psychic, intuition, imagination, interpretation, spiritual nature and perception. Its colour is indigo, a mix of blue and red.

Number seven is the Crown, top of your head. This one deals with the God source, spiritual, intellectual, consciousness, awareness, knowledge and wisdom; sometimes seen as the colour violet or a combination of colours. Its colour is white.

An advanced individual who has full knowledge and awareness of the Chakras and its energies need to start going within through meditation; this will enable you to gain full control of the power they possess. If you were able to tape a meditation focusing on your chakras, (once you feel advanced enough) then please do so. Never forget to close your chakras at the end of your meditation and never forget to say your protection prayer before you start to meditate.

A protection prayer goes something like this.

Great Divine Spirit
As I sit and meditate on my chakras
protect me and surround me with your infinite white light.
Guide me safely as I open each one individually
so that I may experience the powers they embrace
Bring on my awareness as I breathe in each colour
and feel the energy they possess. Amen

When you feel assured and has a companion or two to form a spiritual developing group here's an exercise to follow. Unfortunately one may not get to meditate on this as one needs to be the leader, unless you pre tape it.

Remember the Chakra areas and their colours.

Once you're aware of your higher self, start visualizing each one in sequence, starting from end of spine to top of head.

Concentrate on Chakra number one; bring your attention to the base of the spine. See it opening and sending forth the colour red filling the room and surrounding you. Feel the colour red entering your lungs as you breathe it in and visualize your whole body as red.

Concentrate on Chakra number two, the Sacral—over the genitals. Imagine and sense it opening and sending forth the colour orange, filling the entire room. Breathe in the colour orange and visualize your whole body filled with orange.

Concentrate on Chakra number three, the Solar Plexus—over the abdomen. See it opening and filling the room with yellow. Breathe in the colour yellow and visualize your whole body filled with yellow.

Concentrate on Chakra number four, the Heart—over the centre chest. See it opening and filling the room with green. Breathe in the colour green and visualize your whole body filled with green.

Concentrate on Chakra number five, the Throat—over the larynx. See it opening and filling the room with blue. Breathe in the colour blue and visualize your whole body filled with blue.

Concentrate on Chakra number six, the Brow—centre forehead. See it opening and filling the room with indigo. Breathe in the colour indigo and visualize your whole body filled with indigo.

Concentrate on Chakra number seven, the Crown—top of the head. Visualize it opening and filling the room with white. Breathe in the colour white and visualize your whole body being filled with this loving fluorescent white.

Once you've opened all your Chakra stay within your meditation. Experience the power and feel the energy that's within you. Be aware of any contact you may have with spirit.

Once your meditation time is up, be sure to visualize each and every one of them closing, starting with number one. Take your time and closed them in sequence. (As I visualize each one closing I firmly cap it with a screw on cover, covering each one for self-security.)

Chapter Six
Guardian Angels

Angel Guidance

Dear Angels:
When I walked hand in hand with you, my eyes finally
opened
Your tender voices cheered me as we're heavenward bound
You're leading me on the path of God's White Light
While your soft hands cover my mortal grasp
you firmly hold my soul as we walk to a higher source
The chains that held me to earthly sorrows have been lifted
Doubt binds my soul no more
We're journeying to the loftiest Spirit in the higher realms above.
Amen

The two beautiful children you see below are still on the earth plane. They are my best friend's twin daughters. When I took this picture I saw the true angel likeness they both possess. These two young ladies have so much love and compassion for their friends, family and each other. It's a great feeling of tranquility just to be within their vibration. You'd know when in their company that they're two of God's chosen to be just where they are. I thank God for the wonderful privilege to be a part of their lives.

Angel, according to Webster's dictionary means *a spiritual being superior to man in power and intelligence: one in the lowest rank in the celestial hierarchy, an attendant spirit or guardian, a white-robed winged figure of human form in fine art, a person like an angel (as in looks or behaviour), and one who aids or supports with money or influence.*

My inner understanding of an Angel is that I consider it to be a celestial being and a messenger, or intermediary between God and human. Relatives and friends in spirit may very well be our helpers, guardians and protectors acting as angels in a spirit form. We all have our Angels looking over us and caring for us. We all have an assigned angel prior to birth and this angel has chosen to be our Guardian Angel throughout our lifetime. Those guardian angels could very well be a family relative that had passed to spirit several years before our birth. Those that had evolved close to perfection and are more then capable of being a spiritual parent from the celestial. They had arranged

God's gift to me, on May 25th/02, @ 1148 AM
Picture taken Sept.14th, 2002

with God to take on that amazing task of watching over us while we're in a material existence. Guardian Angels and Celestial Beings are totally opposite. When someone dies they don't become Angelic Angels but some are given the option of being a guardian, taking on angel like qualities by watching over humans while living on earth. We all have freedom of choice and sometimes we go against the advice of our guardians. Later on we become aware of that and realized that we did not listened to that small inner voice once again.

Most religions are concerned with the relationship humans have with the supernatural realm. Your Guardian Angel can function as a protective guardian; such as a heavenly warrior and even as a cosmic power. Angels can be described as personified powers, mediating between the divine and you.

In traditional Israel angels were assumed to have the form of human males, and as a consequence were sometimes mistaken for men. Even to this day we often hear of people seeing human like forms helping them out in an accident when no other person is around. Later on they refer to them as an Angel or such as Jesus or the Blessed Mother Mary. In the 1990s there was a phenomenal amount of popular interest in angels. This interest manifested itself into diverse phenomena. People were buying all they could on Angelic Awareness and wanted to get as much information on the subject as possible. Their eyes had finally opened to what some religions always known about for years. Most of the world began to realize that there's a spiritual being assigned to watch over and guide us from birth.

In my heart, I feel a personal guardian in the spirit world, your Guardian Angel and your Spirit Guides work hand in hand more frequently than we realize.

A friend of mine went to England and visited a Spiritual painter. Apparently he quietly says a prayer and connects with a spirit who was a painter in his material life. (He has no ability to paint himself.) He sees the spirit guide or guardian above the subject's head and then paints the picture. I was very taken with my friend's painting of her guardian. She found an exact photograph of the spirit he had painted. This woman, her guardian, is her great grandmother on her mother's side and the similarities were phenomenal. I got this painter's email address and asked him how else was he able to do a painting, especially for someone like me who had no intentions of travelling to England in the near future. He said that I should take a photo of myself and send it to him. He's able to do it that way. A friend and I did that while my other friend obtained a money order in pounds, and off both photos went. We waited about six-weeks and then the envelope we were both waiting for finally arrived. I didn't want to open it until my friend came by but it took about a week for her to be able to make the trip, so I decided to open it after three days' wait. I was surprised and also a little disappointed to find that I had a guardian instead of a spirit guide but this man's face looked so familiar. I recognized him as a man I met in a meditation while he was working on the railroad but he was much younger then. I was actually introduced to him in a half asleep and half-awake state in a meditation one evening. I felt myself falling asleep in my meditation and I heard a voice say, "Follow me." I felt comfortable and unafraid. I felt the love coming from this spirit so I decided to go along with him. He was leading me through an old ancient house that looked familiar. As he reached and opened the door, a light shone through, he turned around and smiled at me. With that he disappeared. I wondered who he was and why only this and not more. I found out the reason when his photo finally came to me from the spirit painter in England. This envelope also contained a letter saying that he is a guardian and he feels that he's associated with the military as well as with the railroad. As time went by I understood why my guardian was with me at this time. I had the worst month of my life with severe attacks of dizziness and vertigo due to my incurable illness that I have no choice but to live with. I spent up to sixteen hours in bed with dizziness at a time and didn't know if it was ever going to get any better. As time went by I finally accepted and even liked my guardian. Once I learned to accept him I finally decided to try to find out who this gentleman would be. I sent a picture of him to my sister so she could take it to my oldest aunt on my dad's side. My aunt said he looked familiar but she couldn't place him.

The only other person would be my mother. She was away at this time and I had to wait for her return to visit. Somehow I knew my grandmother on my mom's side would know who he was but she has gone to spirit and I'm sure her two youngest children would not have kept any old photographs belonging to her. That's just how they were and one can't change that. When my mother finally visited we had lunch and caught up on the chitchat first. I eventually brought my painting to show her. I said, "Do you know who this is?" She said, "Well now, he looks so familiar with a wrinkled forehead, the familiar nose, a small mouth and his big ears." With that she covered the upper half of his face with a sheet of paper then the lower half. She proceeded to cover the right side of the photo, observed it and then did the same with the left. She said, "I know that face and need a few minutes to place it, give me time." With that I placed the picture in the sunroom with her so she could glance at him periodically. Within about 10 minutes she said, "Mom, (meaning my grandmother) had a picture of him hanging in the living room when I was a little girl." She said it's her mom's Uncle Ambrose. This gentleman in the painting was my great, great uncle. She said that he worked with the railroad as a conductor, went to war, and upon returning he once again took up his position with the railroad. That gave me the verification I was looking for. I'm happy to finally know who he is; and thank you for being my guardian Great, Great Uncle Ambrose. I now know the reason why you presented yourself to me twice before your photo arrived. God Bless you.

My Guardian

Our Spirit Guides are around but I wasn't as much aware of mine as I was my guardian until recently. It's a world of natural flow for them. Once you trust in the love and the power of God you'll be able to make contact and communicate with them more easily. Maintain a healthy and positive outlook.

Guide, as found in Webster's dictionary means: *Direct in a way or course, or show the way to be followed. Influence, superintend, instruct, also implies intimate knowledge of the way and of all its difficulties and dangers. Show the way and often keeping those that follow under control and in order. An*

ability to keep to a chosen course and stresses the capacity of manoeuvring correctly. Last but not least, *guidance by one who finds ways to avoid or overcome difficulties in achieving an end or carrying out a plan.*

There was a Spirit Guide artist going to be at the local church on one Saturday afternoon. I went. I decided I wanted to see my

Spirit Guide and have a picture of him as well. For some reason I knew it would be a male. I watched this woman as she put herself into a trance state and began to draw. Her style and perfection with her hands were unbelievable. I anxiously waited for my turn to come. When it did I went to sit on the chair close to her; she said, "Hold my hands." She held them for about ten seconds and let them go. She picked up her colours and proceeded to draw as she did this with precision and accuracy. I was quite taken aback with her work and at the speed she was able to do it. Her eyes were closed all the time.

My Spirit Guide drawing was finally done. She showed it to me and I was more than pleased at the results, and to find such a wonderful looking gentleman looking back at me. That picture was sprayed and put aside with the rest to dry. While the group of us were standing admiring the photo's I asked the Minister of the church what vibrations she felt from my guide. She said, "He's Mongolian looking, obviously a preacher or a worker of God with the collar and clothes he's wearing." I asked her if she felt there was a name to go along with that. She went silent, closed her eyes for a moment and said, "Mohaws."

Hello Mohaws, thank you for being one of my Spirit Guides and for serving me well. God Bless you.

My Spirit Guide

One morning after my shower, quite sometime after this drawing was done, the mirror was fogged with steam. All of it, all accepts the picture you see above, the one known as my Spirit Guide. There was a design of him as plain as the nose on your face, on the mirror. What stood out the most were the three circles of the vest he's wearing, they were exact. When I saw

this I knew I had the verification I needed. I now know he had presented himself to me to verify; yes that's who I am.

I feel we have more then one spirit-guide. Your guides will change as you progress and move up the ladder of spiritual development. Your first guide will be at the level of your beginning development and will teach you what they know. When they had taught you a certain amount of knowledge you

91

move up another scale and your guide will change as if changing of the guards. The next guide will take over where the other left off. He/she will teach you a more advanced knowingness as if you were in grade school, which I feel this is what it resembles. At this stage of my development I have a new guide. Mohaws has done a great job and also remains with me.

Those of us who choose a spiritual path begin a journey of inner growth and learning. As you become more in tune with the world around you you're also developing emotionally. Some say angels are immortal, ageless and sexless. Sometimes I question the sexless part because of the different energies that I feel. Some feel masculine, some feel very feminine, depending on how the force is presented and received. You too will experience this with development.

You may call on any angel you wish and those that you call on will be more then willing to help. Don't forget to listen within for the answer or recognize that solution that may be, just around the corner. Stay alert and notice the assistance offered and given.

One with Spirit

When the eagle fly's happily with the dove—we'll sense a special love.
We'll be as close to our guardians and angels—as we're ever going to be.
We'll know that the fairy tales have long been left behind.
We'll be enveloped with the energy of pure love, as we too will be as one—with spirit.
Embrace it—and let it shine.

As you live from day to day, you're not aware of who's watching over you or silently standing by your side. Sometimes you may feel there's something-mystical happening when you're in trouble and need God's assistance. As it's mystical, it's spiritual and coming from someone angelic enough to be a guide, a guardian or an angelic being who's with you every moment of your life.

Respect the existence of your Guides, Angels and Guardians. Be assured that a holy intelligence is present at your side and will be forever with you—your minister's of light.

No matter how great your solitude may be— remember, you're never alone.

Chapter Seven
The Afterlife and OBE

OBE Gratitude

God, Holy Divine Spirit:
You guided my spirit we traveled through time
My soul so small in your heavenly realm
The essence of green on the foliage below
The sky cloudless blue as onward we go
You showed me small children as family relations
Two schools all rainbow colours of our nations
Slain animals were waiting to cross the veil
Covered in a white sheet, so no one could tell
Of the way they suffered as they were slain
To provide man's food back on the earth plane
Thank you for giving me a tour of my home
Where I'll meet my loved ones and never be alone
My soul felt at peace, I wanted to stay
You said time would bring that special day.
Amen.
(Based on a personal OBE)

What do we know about it? We know many things from gathered research and medium-ship demonstrations. I did some research so that I could share with you what I have learned.

To describe afterlife it would be an impossible task because of my understanding it's mystical. A place without substance seemingly full of ghosts, angels, spirits and other apparitions, and some people say it's a dream world; but who's responsible for all the unexplainable phenomena? This place does exist. It's the spirit world, the afterlife; in theory it's beyond the human senses. It's so beyond comprehension that it's dismissed as fantasy. It defies all logic; not often rationally explained but we as a spiritual being knows it's there.

Webster's dictionary says that the meaning of afterlife is *an existence after death and a later period in one's life.* **A later period in one's life,** meaning life continues after what we call death?

Many people understand that there's a spirit world but find it difficult to explain. The average person doesn't want to talk about it but hopes it exists.

Deathbed experiences had been examined and recorded over the years by many doctors, certain religious groups and others.

People that had witnessed this had passed this information on to those that had the interest in knowing for documentation.

I've read many books on near death experiences and out of body experiences because I could relate to them. For all of this I was absolutely amazed at all the wonderful things I've read and what I believe to be actual fact. Those factual events were recorded and published by highly educated men and women with university degrees.

Doctor Raymond Moody studied deathbed experiences and approached patients after they had a cardiac arrest or another reason why their heart stop beating, making them clinically dead. Dr. Moody wrote a book with Doctor Melvin Morse and Paul Perry called *"Closer to the light."* I think that was his 4th. In this book, a man that had a near death experience said, *"I learned that life is precious and death is nothing to be feared. We're all born with the knowledge we need to solve life's problems. The answers are all inside if we can just climb over our egos."*

Further on he writes about a nurse that had worked with children. She said after her own experience with the light and listening to the children speak about their happenings that, "Many children and adults have said that their near death experience made them more sensitive to people around them. The messages given to these children are not new or controversial." These messages are:

Love your neighbour and cherish life.

Clean up your own mess.

Contribute to society.

Be the best that you can be.

Be nice, kind and loving.

Do unto others, as you would have them do unto you.

In Dr. Raymond Moody's book called 'Reunion', I found a piece of information that said, *"Studies suggest that as many as 66% of widows experience apparitions of their departed husbands."* I also read that somewhere else. I know for a fact that my younger sister has had such an experience. Her husband passed at a very young age and she grieved deeply, almost to a point of breakdown. His spirit came to comfort her more then once. She was somewhat shocked but gain comfort in his concern beyond the grave.

In Brad Steiger's book called 'Shadow World' he says, *"Accounts of ghostly manifestations, regardless of how frightening they may be, demonstrates that life exists in more than one dimension of reality."*

How true.

Energy can't be destroyed and at the brink of death psychic energy separates itself from the material body to begin a new existence in a higher spiritual dimension. Therefore while we're still on the earth plane the more we use our psychic sense the more it will grow, it's like any other gift.

Brad Steiger also says, *"The world of the supernatural can reach out at any time and envelop any one of us. It matters not who it has signalled out to summon across its borders, for the supernatural is no respecter of persons. Whether we be rich or poor, college educated or street-smart, common labourer or white collar professional, we are all pilgrim souls in an uncharted land when we journey into the dimension of the unknown."*

In your moments of solitude listen and there's one thing you should never forget. The spirit world, the afterlife, is also a home to creatures of darkness as well as beings of light. Always ground and protect yourself with God's white light of protection whenever you decide to meditate or try to make a spirit connection. Recognize the approach of any bad or evil entity and send it away immediately. Be firm with your rejection and don't be afraid, you have Divine Spirit as well as your guardians and angels behind you.

Some time ago an article was placed in my hand. I skimmed over it quickly and liked its contents. I said it was very well written; he said that I could have it. I took it home and picked it apart. The presentation was very educational, to say the least. When I saw this man again I asked him if I could quote him, he gave me a funny look and said, *"What are you quoting me on,"* I told him and then he said, *" Yes, you may quote me"*, Here's what caught my interest. He said, *"Life is a game and it has rules, these rules are natural laws that govern the universe and all that exists within it. It's impossible for us to fully understand the magnitude of the relationship between—God and Soul."*

Quote from a wonderful Medium; Mr. Norman Galka, Oshawa, Ontario, Canada.

In a book called 'Spirit Teachings' by Rev. Stainton Moses, his guide Imperator says *"You shall know that they whom you call dead are alive amongst you; living as they lived on earth, only more really; ministering to you with undiminished love"*.

From my perspective and personal experiences, death itself is beautiful. There's a great feeling of peace that's extremely pleasant. Some may hold a different opinion, which is your soul right.

Your soul has eternal awareness, eternal consciousness, eternal wisdom and eternal existence. At the end of life, your material world, prior to the spirit world, the afterlife, you look back and wonder. Life appeared short and you question about where the time had gone so quickly. Then you realize it was but like a flash of lightning.

Think positively, there's a power much greater. Acknowledge that there is nothing that you and Gods helpers can't achieve together.

Gathered from my own personal experience of an 'out-of-body experience' (OBE) is a departing of your spiritual body from your physical body. While this is happening you're able to observe yourself and your surroundings from outside of your material body. This sort of happening has always been quite common and people are beginning to talk about their experiences more than ever. It's not a hushed situation anymore for the pure fact that it's a part of our self, experiencing the spiritual world and getting a glimpse into our next realm of existence. There are many ways to experience an OBE; drugs, anaesthetic, car accident causing trauma or just having a mild attack of dizziness and vertigo such as I did. I didn't find myself going up or down a tunnel; I literally floated up towards the ceiling and didn't look back. I felt so at peace and protected and I didn't have the need to observe my body below. I knew very well where I was and went along for an experience of a lifetime. My astral travel has opened a new door to my consciousness, one I'll never forget.

As you know by now I have a chronic inner ear problem that affects the nerves and a continuous loss of hearing, frequently causing dizziness and vertigo. Sometimes the attacks are very severe, but this particular one was fairly mild.

One morning as I was having an attack I had to go to my bed and lie down, as I always have to do. I have no choice but to stay there until it runs its course and dies down. While I was lying there for a short while, was as if I went totally within my subconscious and met a spirit who took me on an experience that will remain with me forever. I felt my Spirit/Soul leave my body. It floated above me and I didn't look back. I went with my Guide and we were traveling at a slow speed. I was still in a lying position because I could see my feet. I was as naked as the day I was brought into the world and asked for covering because I felt a little embarrassed. I was told there's no need for embarrassment but I was granted a pair of trousers. As I took another look we were now upright and traveling over green lush grassy fields. I seem to be a lot smaller at this point and we were travelling very close to the ground going between large long thick iris leaves that looked very elegant, tall and beautiful.

My guide never showed himself to me and I didn't ask but his presence was felt so vividly. I didn't need proof of his existence. I knew he was there just from the feel of his loving vibration. He seems to have taken me on a guided tour. I felt perfectly safe and at peace. I felt his love and protection all around me and I couldn't have been more comfortable then a baby in its mother's arms. He took me to a large green field where there were numerous children playing, children of all races and colours. A large building was in the background and I was told it was a school. I went to one little boy of about 6 years of age, gently pinched his cheek and said, "You are a beautiful child." I felt his response of gratefulness and his warm feeling of love. Somehow I felt I knew this little boy.

I was then taken from there to another schoolyard with as many children as the first one. I was told that there are a lot of children on the other side who need to be educated and cared for and that I would most likely be one of the teachers or caretakers when I pass into the spirit world. That pleased me because I love children.

I was then taken to a road, which looked more like a well-used path; it was in a forest and it went through a park. I was shown three adults. Two of the adults, a man and a woman, were with a woman who appeared a little hesitant, nervous and frightened. I had a feeling that they were past loved ones who were close by waiting to guide her along the way. I questioned what was happening. Then I was shown a young woman lying in a hospital bed dying. She was being told that it's ok, don't be afraid, you're perfectly safe and everything is going to be all right. She eventually went.

I was then escorted to another area where all I could see was a lot of white sheets thrown all over the ground covering something. I took a long look at this and sent a telepathic message to my guide and said, "Oh my goodness, there's a dark side here." He said, "No wait, take a closer look and observe."

I did as he advised and noticed that the forms under the white sheets were not of humans as I first expected, they were animals. I kept watching and one of the animals got up, it was either a large dog or a goat, something that size. It walked to my right and out of sight with the sheet still on it. I was told that because of so many animals being slaughtered in the world they have to wait a short time to cross over. There are so many of them it takes a little longer to get through, but they all eventually will.

It seemed to have abruptly ended and I felt that I had been shown enough, all which was intended for me at this given time. I was then asked to return. I felt so at peace and so much love, I didn't want to come back. I felt I was letting my body die there on the bed and I felt my breath relaxing. It was about to cease when my guide said, "No, not yet, this isn't your time, and you have to go back." I felt my spirit, my soul enter my body once again and as I opened my eyes I said, "Wow, what an experience."

Don't always feel you have a choice to leave your body. I wasn't given an actual choice at all. I was told I had to go back, I wasn't asked if I'd like to stay.

After this experience I found myself more open and able to talk willingly about death. My acceptance of death and dying has opened a new door for me. I'm more than willing to help, give guidance and consoling to anyone whom needs it. I've become more loving, kinder, and much more understanding of what happens after we leave our world of learning behind.

I had spoken to a couple of my relatives and told them about this experience. I told them that if ever they find me not breathing please don't be alarmed because if the other side is as wonderful as I had been shown then I'm not coming back if the decision is finally mine to make.

Chapter Eight
Dreams or Astral Travel

Remembering

The time we spent was short and sweet
If not by divine plan how would we meet
You touched a place within my heart
It went so deep it tore apart
A door that's been closed to someone like you
But now it's ajar what will I do
These feelings have surfaced what shall I say
But wish you happiness every day
Would celebrate life's event with you
Situations stop me as they usually do
I'll visit again to hold you tight
Hug you close with all my might
I may not let go for what have you done
Within my eyes you're part of the sun

Every day living as an adult deals mostly with working five days a week and a two-day rest period before back to the grindstone, so to speak, for another five days. Seems like a never ending battle—but we have to work if health permits, for survival and to rear and educated our children the best we possibly can. Sometimes somewhere along the way we tend to take our loved ones, friends, and life itself for granted. I've heard many people say over the years or have asked the question or just to make a comment, *"what is life all about,"* and *"what is the purpose of living?"* You get those questions when someone is down-and-out or have suddenly lost a love one to spirit. Those words are usually the words of people who had not been properly educated about the spirit world and the continuation of life after death. Life is precious and from the beginning to the end, birth to physical death, is the cycle or the circle of life. Within this life cycle we have frequent connections with the spirit world. Sometimes when we express our experiences we're being told that we're dreaming or we're going crazy and should see a shrink. I remember being told this a few times in my childhood until I realized enough to keep my mouth shut and to keep my amazing experiences to myself.

Not having proper access to the right information or being of an organized religion that doesn't teach life after death—we are ignorant to this. No one's to blame firsthand because this had been past down from generation to generation. Eventually I was able to express my experience at any time when I met a woman 20 years ago who listened intently to my stories. She believed and respected my experiences and I willingly shared them with her. She's still a wonderful friend and although she's 20 years my senior we're like brother and sister. When I sometimes get a little down and question whether I should continue my spiritual path she's the first one to encourage me not to give up. She encourages my continuance by bringing up some of my past expressed experiences.

A lot of our spiritual experiences happened when we sleep at night or when in a slight meditation such as sitting quietly alongside of the ocean listening to the waves hit the shore. I did this often as a child. What beautiful memories they are now because I found the right channel that guided me to the spiritual side that I somehow always knew was there.

When you sleep your mind is at work and very active. Dreams are clues to daily existence. That which you experience in dreams is but a small speck of what you're capable of experiencing in the universe. Is it dreams we're actually having or is it something special way beyond our human imagination? Sometimes you may have awakened and thought or said, "Wow— *That was too real to be a dream.*"

When you question this it was probably too real to be a dream, therefore possibly making it an out-of-body experience or a spiritual travel contact in the astral plane. Dreams are answered to our many questions, one needs but to interpret them correctly. Being a medium and oftentimes interpreting symbols, given from the spirit world, one is capable of dream interpretation. Like mediumship, this too can be taught.

Were you ever in a situation where your life flashed before your eyes? This usually happens in life threatening circumstances. This had happened to me a few times as a child. For example; I'd get a few friends together and look for the highest and sometimes the steepest hill that we could find in the area, which was a mountain to a child, and we'd try to climb it. On a few occasions one or two of us would stumble, slip or be hanging on for dear life to keep from falling and then more often then not the one in that situation would have a life review. On many occasions I've heard someone say, *"My life just flashed in front of my eyes";* although we were frightened beyond belief we liked this wonderful experience. We were very proud to tell our other friends, that didn't come that day, of our adventures. Were we closer to God at those times? It felt absolutely amazing and now as I look back I feel that we were one with the light for a moment or two. A moment or two is all it takes for a life review.

Have you ever wondered about your soul, whether you have one or not? You don't possess a soul—you are soul; you, the soul but in a human body having a material lifetime experience.

One night when you go to bed ask out loud for insight and solutions to problems or ask for help in having a conscious out-of-body or a spiritual-astral-plane-experience, SAPE. You may remember that before you sleep you sometimes have concerns about something; and as you sleep there it is, with you. From your time in the astral, or your dream state if you prefer, you've come up with an answer or was given a solution by a higher being of light.

Each night pray for assistance and protection before going to sleep and ask for this experience to happen when the need is there. Try to get past the feeling of being afraid and be certain that you are as safe as you are here on earth. From personal experiences your astral travel guide won't let you down.

If you decide to try this, here's one exercise to follow. Before going to sleep, ask for assistance to astral travel. Pray to God, your guardian angels and your guides. Be firm in your request and almost demand that you'll remain aware of the experience after awakening, as many times we travel and forget. Or do as a couple of my friends; set your clock to alarm around midnight, but if you don't set it and happen to wake during the night and would like to give it a try follow these instructions. Go to bed and sleep; when you awake by alarm or otherwise stay up for a short while. Not to long or you'll become to alert and have a problem getting back to sleep. When you go back to bed make the Om, Um, Em, Hem or a variety of sounds or just hum an inspirational song or hymn; or chant a low quiet humming sound that sounds inspired to you. Hum softly so you won't wake others in the house. If you prefer use any other spiritual sound that's peaceful to your ears and drift back to sleep. Actually any sound will work if you believe in it. It's possible that you will have a wonderful experience like astral travel. If this happens you'll most definitely become aware of the fact that you're not dreaming and recognize the soul's spiritual ability and focus on its needs.

There are many levels of consciousness, the physical being the lowest, the astral, casual, mental and etheric just to name a few. I heard someone say at some point that the etheric level is associated with water slapping gently on the shoreline or a buzzing sound, and another said it sounds like soft peaceful wind chimes. Guess it depends on the individual and where they are in their spiritual growth. I hadn't experienced any such sounds in a SAPE other then what is of the normal on the earth plane, but I had in a deep meditation.

Don't fear if and when adventuring into the many levels of the astral because they're a natural part of your existence, a part that you're only aware of in the sub-conscious.

When you've developed enough confidence and you'd like to continue the dream state of, quote on quote, an out of body 'spiritual' experience through astral travel, the first thing you may become aware of is the spiritual evolution of your soul; you'll automatically know that you've moved to a higher state of being. Don't attempt or try experimenting with God's Light during your first experiences; you'll be too amazed and to busy to try and keep up with your guide anyway to even give this a thought. That will eventually come with a lot of effort and astral travel experiences. If you do see a bright light in the distant remain from travelling towards it until you're more assured of what you're doing and trusting totally in your guide.

With experience you'll come to the conclusion that you exist quite well and somewhat independently outside of your physical body. Speaking from a personal viewpoint, I say independently but independence comes only after many travels with trusted guides. Faith, love, hate or fear and or anger do not mix and chances are you will experience it somewhat. Whether here in the physical or in the astral, remain faithful to yourself and the god source and be at you achieved maximum level of spiritual advancement. Remember that your astral body is your personal vehicle for the astral plane; it's a copy or a replica of your physical body but considerably smaller in comparison.

Be aware and rid yourself of negative emotions, thoughts and feelings immediately as any attempts made to achieve a higher state of consciousness will be all in vain; meaning practise love and peace continually.

Sometimes while asleep you may experience many feelings such as: falling from a height or traveling backwards causing panic, which causes the body to create a shortness of breath and usually end up with a sudden abrupt awakening with fear. Don't let this stop you from wanting another experience, you'll gain more control with time.

What if you find yourself in darkness? If this happens don't be afraid but look about and you'll see a glimmer of light in the distance, it may appear as a white bright light or a flickering blue-like star, some see it as a speck of brightness. Whatever the case, speak to your guide and ask for light. Tell your guide that you want to see what's happening; this always works for me. You're safe; God is closer than ever, feel protected.

How about flying in your sleep? Did you ever experience this? I've done this on many occasions as a child and had thoroughly enjoyed it. I knew some of my childhood dream-like-experiences weren't a farce and that they were as real as astral travel could possibly get. Now as an adult I request for this to happen, which it does and oftentimes automatically; I wake with such a feeling of elation. Sometimes you may have awakened and had the feeling of a state of paralysis. This happened to me only once and it was frightening. I was calmed down by a loving force; I relaxed and went back to sleep. I was also told, telepathically, that I was ok and that sleep would take care of the fear I'm having and it would rid me of it. With further spiritual growth I now know how to handle this if it should ever happen again.

The power of thought needs to be used wisely, especially when experiencing the astral plane where deceased loved ones and or strangers will present themselves without warning or been called upon. There's nothing more powerful then that of your mind so take advantage of your thoughts when sudden appreciations appear, either in the astral or on the earth plane. Remember, if you achieve the SAPE and your guide gives you control, only then be certain that you dominate and guide your travels but never send your guides away, they are your protectors.

Not all out of body experiences have been planned and one doesn't have to be clinically dead to have one; they may just automatically happen where humanoid figures will be encountered. They're your overview caretakers and guides that will try to communicate with you. They won't be able to do this if you're afraid. Try your utmost to suppress your fear and raise your vibration level to meet theirs; this is also done by mediums when spirit connection is made. This you'll learn through meditation and progressive experience when doing the meditation exercises at the back.

If you hear a voice that you don't feel comfortable with when contacting spirits on the astral plane, they will detect it and most often lower the tone to a more non threatening level.

It may even change from a male to female and possibly as low as a whisper so that you'll be more comfortable. Gently calm yourself as they want you to be as comfortable and relaxed as possible. They are of love and want your respect and trust.

An individual that has passed on and not realized it often refuse to accept the fact of death; then he/she may continue to haunt the place of residence or a place that had meant a lot to him/her while alive. Even some that died suddenly by accident will continue to reside at the place of physical death creating ghost like visions, seen by many. Give this some thought, what if you suddenly found yourself in another part of the world and couldn't speak the language and everyone ignored you? That is the same for those that had died and hadn't realized it or refuse to accept it. Sometimes it angers them and the only way they can get attention is by a sudden materialization or frightening people in other ways.

Spirits, Angels and Guides come and go depending on your needs. If you had been spiritually assisted, which all of us have whether we're aware of it or not, then with spiritual knowledge you'll learn how to assist lost souls, especially while in astral travel. This is called soul rescue. If the opportunity arises by all means help those in need. Assist and show them the way 'to the light'. All a lost soul needs is reassurance of physical death and to be informed of life on the other side, that which he had not been educated about while on the earth plane. Practise love and acceptance always, whether in your daily life or astral travel. Love of a mother is usually an unforgettable love; therefore if you call on a lost soul's mother she'll gladly come to receive them and take them 'Across the Vail'.

When I was writing this I got a phone call from a friend. She said, "I have bad news, I got a call this afternoon and was told that a colleague of mine has cancer of the liver, she's only 50 years old. They say that for every death there's a birth." I replied saying, "You're correct in saying this because at the onset of death the body is reborn in the spirit world, therefore a new birth has begun." What she was insinuating was that a new earth-life would begin with the birth of a child but she appreciated my point of view and said, *"I never thought of it that way"*.

The physical world is at the lowest of levels and it's actually the less influential in your life; you'll eventually realize and come to terms with this in your spiritual development. Although we're on earth we're not of it, as the bible says. The body returns to the dust over time such as all living things but the real you, your soul, is of the incredible and powerful spiritual beings here on earth having a human experience.

Astral means, of the stars, and from personal experience I do believe that once leaving the physical we are exactly that. You too will find yourself capable of journeying light years through space and maybe even time. Recently I have been time travelling but back in time not forward. This is an amazing experience as it shows that life is continuous and reincarnation is probable. Continue to practise and sense that you're guided by the power of thought and you'll eventually gain power to manoeuvre your travels and chosen destinations. This will be granted to you only once your guides feel that you're capable to fully designate and control.

You'll leave your physical body simply through the thought process, so it will appear. Once left the physical and you have the control, direct yourself to a room with a mirror and you'll notice that you won't see a reflection, like that of a ghost; unless you have evolved to a higher spiritual level and gained such a powerful train of thought that you'll project one in your consciousness. Oftentimes you won't know where you're going until much practise but always be aware that you'll travel where your thoughts are directed. You have to condition yourself to think like a spiritual being which may be very hard to do at first. Furthermore, as a beginner you're not always aware of where you're travelling as your personal guides are the director and the controller.

You'll appear much different in the astral plane, such as that in dreams but take notice and see that you're no larger then a speck of sand, if that. Your travel will respond instantaneously such as that of an UFO, you see it and within a moment it disappears. Rely on your higher self to create stability and rid yourself of any fear that you're most likely to sense until you feel safe within it. Reassure the imminent by trusting in God, your guardians and most of all, your guides.

In the summer of 2003 something extra-ordinary happened to me, one of many over the years. When it first happened I was a little concerned that there may be something wrong with my vision as my sight was being affected. But being developed spiritually to a higher level than the normal I knew better then to have fear. I could sit back anywhere, anytime, and once relaxed enough I could see hundreds of spirit beings in front of my 'opened' eyes. I would call them my angels. I was doing just that one-day while I was sitting in the car waiting for my brother. Once he arrived I explained to him what I was seeing, he listened but said nothing. I thought '*Silence is golden*'. They appeared to be about 1/8 inch in length and very thin and wiggly. They appeared as minute beings of light swimming around in astral space such as that of moving tadpoles in crystal clear water. To explain further, they looked like thousands of tadpoles swimming back and forth amongst each other without colliding.

I may have questioned their reality but I saw them with eyes open, not closed. I was able to control when I wanted to experience this and I found comfort in my day when I did. My astral friends stayed around and can be easily located when called on.

Phenomenon such as this and some of your own personal experiences, that you may have refuse to accept as fact, represents a glimpse of a much wider universe open to everyone. If you're reading this book you're probably one of those people that are capable of experiencing this if you haven't already done so.

Keep in mind that you have a subconscious connection with the All, and that 'you' are a spark of God, a spark of the divine.

'With God all things are possible', The Holy Bible, New Testament in the book of Matthew 19:26

Chapter Nine
Spiritual Healing

Protection Prayer

Divine Heavenly Father.
Accept me as an instrument of light.
Make me a clear channel for those light ones who walk
beside me that we may work together to bring peace, comfort
and healing to those in need.
Let's show the world that there's no death beyond our earth
life existence. Please protect me against any negative
vibrations that will try to interfere in my goal of goodness.
Amen

(Jose Padial, Spain.)

First of all, you have to have faith in yourself and in God.
When you have faith you have mind energy that is very, very
powerful. If you need help to attune and connect with your
healing guide or guides you may need to study the Seven
Principles of a Spiritualist Church and or the Ten
Commandments or the guidelines of a loving spiritual

organization. All religions have such as this or similar ethical standards. Try your best to live by it in order to help develop your mind power to build the faith you need to give proper spiritual healing.

Faith is a conviction deep within a state of certainty of reassurance. When you feel deeply you create an enormous amount of energy.

Faith as found in Webster's dictionary means, *allegiance to duty or a person, fidelity to one's promises, sincerity of intentions, belief and trust in and loyalty to God, belief in the traditional doctrines of a religion, firm belief in something for which there is no proof, complete trust, something that is believed especially with strong conviction and a system of religious beliefs.*

My personal understanding of what is meant by faith in this perspective is to believe and have complete trust in God.

Purification of the mind is one of the main principles and it's the first step necessary to give Spiritual Healing. You accomplish this through Prayer and asking God for assistance and direction. The centre of Divine Intelligence and Wisdom, God, seems to release deeper mental and spiritual levels. As you work with energy through a mental process an interaction between God and your healing guides will bring you into an attunement that will make you feel energetic, as if energized by a power beyond your control and understanding. Once you ground yourself and feel attunement with your healing guides and God, say a prayer of self-protection. (Example at the beginning of this chapter)

You activate your super consciousness level through spiritual study, meditation, prayer or using affirmations, which awaken this phase of your mind. Most of us know how to pray and meditate. This should be done regularly. If you're unable to do this in the quiet of your own home, find a group you're comfortable with. Attend the gathering regularly and learn how to meditate and pray. If you need guidance on how this is done ask the teacher, who is likely to be a Medium and that person will be only too glad to give you guidance in meditation and talk you through a prayer.

When you have accomplished Faith Healing of yourself, it's time to move on to another person. It's now the time to give healing to others, whether it's a spiritual, physical or mental healing. The best place to start is within the church environment. Some churches teach this as a course of study and some others include it in a gathering in the church where there are willing receivers eagerly waiting to receive.

You need to understand and believe that when you apply the power of thought, you know you're under Divine Law. Then your mind receives the healing power from the God source, which you visualize and project on to the receiver, restoring the body. Never underestimate the great power of thought. Love heals so therefore keep love within your heart at all times. Something as simple as a hug is a transference of energy.

Spiritual healing is not a cure but it initiates a healing source once you open yourself to energy through your guides. You're the instrument between your healing doctors and the person you're healing. If you have a chance, meditate with deep spiritual thoughts prior to this. Speak with God and request His white light of protective healing energy. Feel a divine source close by and speak to God and your guides telepathically as if they were sitting next to you. Once attuned with them set your goal with a focus on body balance. If you know of an affected area that had been discussed prior to healing then make it your central focus point. Your main criteria should be restoring a balance between body and spirit. Consider the problem spoken-of and make it a priority.

There's a divine current within you that carries healing power. Your energy flows where your attention is directed.

Concentrate and envision healing happening. Without any interruptions hold your thoughts and send forth all the healing power that comes from your healing guides, through you, to your receiver. Don't break the connection unless either one of you are in danger. Even in noisy situations remain focused on what you're doing blocking out disturbances through your mind power.

As you deliberately direct your attention and release the flow of energy this calls into action the intelligent principle located in that area of the body and also stimulates energy throughout, and healing results. Give and send healing unconditionally. Some healers feel energy through their heart chakra but whatever way you do it, healing is healing none the less. Healers also need healing sometimes themselves.

There should be a bowl of water present to cleanse your hands and a towel or paper towels for drying. Do this visualizing it removing any negative energy and totally cleansing your mind, body and spirit.

Go to your receiver and stand behind her. (Although I use the feminine pronoun here it refers to all). Speak softly and ask for permission to touch her as government law varies with procedure in physically touching another. Raise your hands chest high, palms upward, close your eyes, call forth your healing guides and say a prayer asking God for the Power and energy to heal the person in front of you. Or you may say an affirmation in place of a prayer.

An Example of an Affirmation Is:

I'm receiving Divine Intelligence and Healing Power from God, my protector and Divine Source. You'll give me the ability to heal this Man or Woman sitting in front of me.

(Put Emphases on Divine Intelligence, Healing Power and God) This affirmation will awaken the power within your super consciousness.

A Prayer Example Is:

Dear God, Divine source, please give me the energy and power, through you, to heal this 'Woman, Man or child' sitting in front of me. Give me guidance and focus healing energy where it's most needed. Amen.

Whichever you choose, visualize the white light power of God entering you from the crown of your head or the back of your neck, whatever is comfortable for you. Then visualize it travelling down your arms and into the person you're healing. You're the instrument that God is using to direct and divert the penetrating source of His healing energy. You may touch this person on both shoulders to start with and visualize a burst of healing energy entering there. Wait for a sensation indicating a balance of energy before moving your hands to the next location. Move both hands in unison over the body while continuing to visualize God's Power moving through you, entering your receiver. It's also recommended to try and cover all the Chakra's of the body except for the crown, which you do not totally cover but encircle it with both hands. Focus on the back of your receiver and be careful not to touch any personal areas. It's recommended that you bring your hands down the spine a total of three times. If taking this course for 'certification in spiritual healing' the teacher will be there to guide you.

While you're giving healing you'll sometimes experience flashes of inspiration and guidance through your super consciousness. As you do your part you're deliberately arousing your mind powers constructively with the help of your guides and the divine source. You can be certain that your subconscious will control the automatic functions of your body and prepare you for the giving of healing.

When you sense a peace of mind, that's when the healing is

setting in. You need not hear, feel or even be aware of it happening, but that peaceful feeling will be all you need to assure you that healing is taking place.

To complete total spiritual body healing, take both of her hands in yours as you stand before her. Put them in a praying hands fashion while you hold and cover them in your praying hands pointing in the opposite direction. Thank God for His help and ask God to take care of her and give her health, strength, guidance and protection. Always tell your receivers God Bless because that's just what has happened.

God has blessed and healed through you.

For the Person Receiving Healing:

When the time comes and you've decided to go to the healing stool, this is what I recommend. Visualize God in your presence. Walk to the healing stool while visualizing God's white protecting light all around you. As you sit down place the back of your hands slightly behind your knees with palms up; then raise them about an inch or so and say a quick prayer asking God for the healing you need.

This prayer could go like this:

Great Divine Spirit, please give me the healing you so desire and direct it to where it's most needed. Amen.

While you're saying your prayer, the healer is most likely praying as well, asking for the energy and power to heal you.

After your personal prayer place your hands on your thighs, palms up, and as you feel the first laying on of hands on your shoulders, feel the flow of energy entering you through that area and feel it course through your entire body. This is the biggest burst of energy that is given.

If you have a particular area you feel needs more attention, direct the energy from one area to the other where you most need it. For instance: if your healer moves her hands to your shoulders and you have a sore knee, visualize the healing energy going through your shoulders directly to your knee.

As her hands move over your body, visualize this procedure all the way through the healing, with a one focused point of directed energy.

Thank her when the healing is completed and then go back to your chair. Sit quietly as you did on the healing stool, close your eyes and thank God for the healing you've just received. Open your eyes when you're ready.

If you feel any tingling in your hands or fingers, that's extra energy from the power source, God and His healers. Rub your hands gently over your thighs and give this energy back to yourself.

Distant and Absent Spiritual Healing:

Distant spiritual healing deals with the power of thought. As we all know, the power of thought is very powerful and not always understood how it works by scientific means through an individual.

When you have an ill friend or family member that's too far away to visit, don't feel you're unable to help them. You can give them distant healing right from your own home. Go through the above purification. Close your eyes and say a prayer asking God for his healing power to enter you so you may direct it to the body and soul of your ailing friend or family member. Visualize yourself receiving God's healing force through the back of your neck or the crown of your head, travelling down your arms into your hands. Open your hands and visualize the healing force of God travelling through them. Visualize it travelling through the atmosphere outside and going directly to the person you're sending it to.

Visualize this healing power as a bright white light, and imagine it spreading all over the person you're sending it to. Remain in this position for the time that feels right for you and then imagine the white light force returning back, but a little duller than what you had sent.

Thank God and your healing guides in a prayer for their help and ask them to continue on giving this healing; you may wish to send another the following day. You're most certainly welcome to send as often as you wish but once a day should be sufficient.

Self Healing:

Follow the exercises mentioned above as if you were going to give and or send healing. This is what you're actually doing but it's to and for yourself. Sit in quiet, close your eyes and say your protection prayer. Firmly believe that God will help you heal yourself through your own sub-consciousness and mindfulness of your own spiritual will power. Visualize the source as a beautiful white glowing light entering you where your problem is and filling you with total blissfulness of healing energy. Imagine the entire predestined touch coming from the hands of God and going directly into you reaching where you had directed it. Affirm yourself that you're recovering from your ailment and truly believe that you are.

A daily affirmation of well being is a great way to start your day.

When you have completed any healing always thank God and your healing guides

God Bless.

Chapter Ten
Trance

A Trance Prayer

Heavenly Spirit of the universe:
Surround me with your bright white light of protection
Guide me inward as I search for you within my higher self
Connect and present my door keep so I may rely on his
guidance
Enlighten my soul with your wonderful knowledge of
existence
Give me peace within and use me as a channel
Comfort and show me the way
Project those from the spirit world, threw me, to serve others.
Amen

Trance according to Webster's dictionary means *a state of partly suspended animation or inability to function, a somnolent state* (as of deep hypnosis) *and a state of profound abstraction or absorption.*

In my point of view trance results in gradual assumption as a form of hypnosis through the power of suggestion, which can be brought on by deep meditation. You the student is brought into a state of consciousness, in which attention is withdrawn from the outside world and is concentrated on mental sensory and psychological experiences.

To accomplish trance you may need to find a doctor who can perform a good hypnosis. Better still, find a teacher who is a doctor and is able to hypnotise and also teach trance.

When a teacher induces trance a close relationship or rapport develops between the teacher and the student. The responses of a trance-student with spiritual phenomena or the behaviour they manifest is objective and is the product of their motivational set; that is, behaviour reflects what is being sought from the experience. Most people can be easily put into trance but have to be a willing participant and want it to happen as well as if you were to be regressed. The depth of a trance varies widely depending on the fears that you may have. A profound trance is characterized by the forgetting of trance events and by an ability to respond automatically to posthypnotic suggestions that are not too anxiety provoking.

With continued practice and experience you'll feel the need to be more in control and eventually feel secure enough for the guide that you brought through to take over completely.

The depth of achievable trance is a relatively fixed characteristic depending on your emotional condition and the skill of a good teacher. Once you get the feel of trance you must always realize that you have to remain in control. Then you may permit an entity, such as your spirit guide, speak through you. You remain in control or this entity may just take over your total body, mind and spirit for a period of time saying what he/she waited to say for a long time. You have to guide and direct while remaining alert enough to gain your control over the entity. You have the greatest power behind you, God. Call on his help and protection before going into this state of consciousness or when you feel the need while there.

It is said that only 20 percent of the people are capable of entering somnambulistic states through the usual methods of induction. I don't agree with this as I had witness higher. I tend to think that any individual is capable of this when all fear is put aside and trust totally in the teacher. Medically speaking, twenty percent is not significant since spirit phenomena effects occur even in a light trance.

Trance can produce a deeper contact with one's emotional life, resulting in some lifting of repressions and exposure of buried fears and conflicts. That's why a lot of hidden hurt and emotions surface at this point in time. This effect potentially lends itself and opens up a door you probably closed a long time ago on things you haven't totally dealt with. Go within and deal with it, get it out of your system so this won't surface again. Therefore your suppressed forgotten memories won't be fused with your spiritual contact.

Here's a little insight to help you combat any fear you may have and feel totally at ease with your experienced teacher. Native Americans generally have shown less interest in an afterlife than have Christian's. Native Americans have traditionally tended to assume that the souls of the dead go to another part of the universe, where they have a pleasant existence carrying on everyday activities. Souls of unhappy or evil persons might stay around their former homes, causing misfortunes but are unable to enter you while guided in trance with the protection of prayer from the God source. Both your own private prayer prior to going into trance and the one given by your teacher, prior to the beginning of the circle, will protect you.

Your moral obligation when you decide to give trance a try

is to trust your teacher and let yourself go and be brought into contact with your Spirit Guide. She or he knows how to control and manage any entity that would like to stay a little longer than they are welcome to. Trust and feel comfortable; you're in safe hands. You'll be directed in patterned ways of interacting with spiritual beings. Such spiritual communication is often the centre of the trance that she or he has so many times put into practice. When you feel your spirit guide within, it's like you're especially dependent on him or subjected to the forces of the universe that are beyond your control. Do not fear; you're having an experience in life that you probably never had before. You're perfectly safe with your leader and within the environment.

In many societies, possession (control of a person's body by a spiritual entity) is a common form of interchanging with the spirit world. Through intensive training your teacher has already acquired the ability to bring you into a trance state and negotiate with spirits, whether it is your guide or not, but most likely it will be. In so-called possession rites, spirits are believed to only enter the bodies of willing candidates.

Relationship with the divine can also be expressed in terms of moral behaviour. This means devotedly adhering to their revealed precepts for conduct and their standards of spiritual life in general. Individuals cultivate a lifelong personal relationship with God, and then grow to love and trust the laws of the universe.

Genuine trance communication is when a spirit teacher comes forward to inspire and instruct. Once able to do this one comes to realize that it's a remarkable experience. When you seek answers from spirit it's with the acknowledgement that there is no greater power than the divine light within each individual. If one is not familiar with this ones ego often stops them from listening to the intuitive voice that speaks from a higher self.

At the beginning of development you'll need assistance in grasping the connection to this gift, the connection that all have but unrecognizable until it's brought to your attention. Spirit teachers cannot read your mind but are able to read the energy of your soul's blueprint and respond to your questions from that perspective. As your teachers teach they'll remind you of everything that is needed for your own personal growth and well being; preparing you to progress for your betterment and the betterment of others.

Genuine trance mediumship is fairly rare as in total control. Its development comes only to those who have, within their mental and physical organisms, a certain type of vital magnetic energy. Spirit uses this energy in order to induce various degrees of control. In this state the Spirit teacher is able to impact directly the body and the consciousness of the medium and speak in a more direct fashion. Certain Spirit teachers will guide and work with you through various phases and stages of your development because spirit teachers change as you progress.

Full control or deep trance is of great value in proving life after physical death and is usually validated immediately by the sitter. The greater control the more pronounced the discarnate.

I personally feel that a spirit teacher can also be someone on the earth plane teaching the student the spiritual aspect of what it all entrails. I couldn't tell you for sure who my spirit teacher is, from the spirit world, but I do know that three different and safe entities had come through in trance in development class.

Silver Birch is a spirit teacher, he's a high being in the spirit world who came to earth for a period of time to serve all of mankind with his teachings. There are many others; and books are available for your means in a form of teaching.

A First Trance Experience

I was guided into trance via suggestion, for the first time, in a development class. The teacher started by reading what trance is all about, its effects on you and what you actually feel while in trance, symptoms and emotions etc. We were told never to touch anyone while in trance no matter what the results are. The teacher has a good sense of humour (when she chooses) and it's a pleasure to hear her wit. She confirmed that she knew how to control the Spirit Guides that come through, so I immediately felt at ease with her assurance which gave me confidence. After the lesson I understood why this shouldn't be done without an experienced teacher. This should only be done with someone who has had proper teaching and experience and knows how to control the guides that come through.

During the lesson some guides were very stubborn and didn't want to leave. Some others informed the teacher that they should leave for reasons that they stated through their medium, such as my guide with feeling my body unwell due to excitable apprehension.

The trance was started by talking the group into a meditation state.

I didn't hear a lot of what was said because of my hearing loss, plus she spoke very softly. I'm so used to meditating I let myself go after I said my protection prayer and visualized God's Protective White Light surrounding me. I then went in to a very deep meditation, totally relaxed and yet totally in her control.

She started to call the Spirit Guides and mine jumped in immediately. I felt the change as my heart started to beat considerably fast; my head felt as if it were pounding with the beats. I got tightness around my neck, and my arms felt so heavy I couldn't lift or move them. I got tingling down my arms to the tips of my fingers, which were throbbing. It was a good feeling although my heart was beating as if I ran a marathon. I didn't get scared but my guide was very anxious and wanted to speak immediately.

By the time my name was called my guide had settled down, but once he heard my name being called and he got permission to return, the same feelings returned and my heart started to race again. He spoke very quietly through me and said, "This is too hard on his heart, and I won't stay long. He has tightness around his neck and I should leave now." He waited until he was thanked for his appearance and was asked to leave. With that I heard the teacher mention my name and said, "Bring yourself back now, bring yourself back. Breathe deeply and come back. Come back, open your eyes." I opened my eyes and found that they were both a little wet in the corners. There was a slight tear in both. I wiped it away.

I immediately looked over at another student who has gone into trance a few times before without the aid of the teacher. I knew she was deep within. She was, as they say, out for the count. She was sagged in her chair with both hands flopped to her side. Eyes closed tight and a face that was slightly distorted. She looked like a stubborn little child pouting to get her own way. I almost laughed out loud at the dear woman, but managed to contain it and held it inside.

When the teacher called her name she was jarred as if a soldier was brought to attention. Her mouth flew open and stayed that way. I had another inner chuckle. When the teacher called on her guides to use her voice box, her guide laughed and said a very slow, Hi. Her mouth didn't move, but remained open. How she spoke is beyond me but the words came out nonetheless. Then again I don't know what I looked like either, maybe someone else was having an inner laugh at me.

We all know that laughter is very good for the soul. Her guide was much like that of a little girl. Laughed a lot and when she was told to leave she said, "Ok. Can I come back again sometime?" The teacher said that she could and the guide said, "Ok, I'll go now then." With that she brought her back to consciousness. When she opened her eyes they were budging out and totally wet with tears. Compared to all of the other students, this woman was definitely the best of all.

There were another couple of people who cried uncontrollably, one while in trance and the other immediately after she was brought back. There was one similar to me. Her Guide said that if he stayed any longer she'd be sick. He first spoke in French and was told to translate into English, which he did.

An interesting evening and so it was. The rest went well. Some were in the previous year's class and had gone into trance before. Their guides came through quickly and were patient with the student-mediums. A couple didn't get to go in trance at all because a little fear was involved. They sat and observed. The teacher told them at the end of the evening that they'd get another try in the following class.

It was a pleasant feeling of awe, although my heart was jumping out of my chest. I asked about the heart pounding and was told that my guide entered through the heart chakra. Good answer I thought.

It's funny, the moment I felt him depart, my heart totally relaxed, quickly.

The Second Trance Experience

My second trance experience was much more peaceful. I was aware when my turn was going to come because the teacher went clockwise and I was the second last to be called upon to allow my guide to come through. As usual the teacher guided us into a beautiful meditation using only half of the group at a time. I was in the first half and went within very quickly; she spent a while relaxing the group through meditation but a few others such as I didn't need quite as long. Some are very new to this and needed that extra calming. My guide let me know very early that he was there and I felt more in control this time and kept him at bay. At one point I felt my heart starting to speed up and I immediately let my guide know what was happening, and he backed away until I was more relaxed. I kept him at a distance and when the teacher got through with the other students I permitted him and felt him fully enter my being. He was much gentler this time around and I felt in control. He responded fairly quickly and was very patient; he waited until he was asked before volunteering anything. When he finally got to use my voice box, I could feel his loving energy and could actually hear what he was saying.

The teacher said, "Good evening, hello friend, welcome."

I felt him trying to speak but he needed a little more energy.

The teacher spoke up again and repeated the same greeting.

This time he finally spoke and said,"Hello and thank you"

The teacher said, "You're welcome, do you have anything to say?"

He said, "Yes"

Then the teacher asked, "What would you like to tell us this evening?"

He said, "I think you all should hear this."

The teacher said, "Go on friend."

He said, "Inner peace brings joy, contentment and harmony, express it with love; you have spiritual guidelines to follow, follow them. I say no more."

The teacher said, "Thank you friend for that wonderful message, I now have to ask you to leave."

Then I heard her call my name to bring me back and I was aware of how heavy my lower arms were and it felt like I was unable to lift them. As she called me back I felt my whole being and heart more relaxed and finally the heaviness left my arms.

When I opened my eyes and was back to reality I observed the rest of the group. The same woman as before, across from me, was well into trance. Her position and facial features indicated that the entity inside waiting was no doubt a military man. The fixed motionless body posture and the stern look on her face indicated it. It was quite some time before the teacher got to her and the entity got fed up waiting. I could tell he was leaving her by her body expression as it was becoming more relaxed by the second and her hand slowly falling to rest on her upper leg. She was in the same fixed position for about 15 to 20 minutes and didn't move a muscle. Once the entity left she totally relaxed, her head lowered slowly at the same time her hand did. I was entranced with the whole situation myself. Unfortunately that entity didn't return and when her name was called she brought through an opera singer and gave us a high opera song that was very pleasant to hear. Some of us had a little inner laugh and some of us actually enjoyed the performance, I know I did. She was brought back to consciousness and when she finally came back it looked like she was about to have projectile vomiting but she controlled herself. She was a little teary eyed but also did very well in her trance. It's amazing how easily your guides will enter your conscious when called upon by a trained and confident leader.

As progression advances with your studies and the work courses and exercises at the end it's possible that trance will eventually occur when you're confident. If you have a group to practise trance, here's an example of granted permission to use you as a sceptre.

Permission

Doorkeeper/highest guide:

I give you permission to allow a spirit entity to speak through me.

I'm ready and willing to channel words of love and wisdom sent forth from the spirit world.

I ask that you continue to keep all negative forces away.

I feel protected and have no fear.

Thank you

Here's a trance meditation to assist you but only with the company of another that has had experience in it. You probably have nothing to fear as inspired speaking in a deep meditation is a lower form of trance.

Meditation: Trance

If you're serious in developing trance I suggest that you use a tape recorder and record your experiences for further development. You may also like to use it as a referral to your progression.

'Protect' meaning ask God to protect you and visualize yourself covered by White Light

'Ground' meaning that you visualize your feet going deep into mother earth as your head is covered with Gods hands.

'Connect' meaning that from deep into mother earth all the way above your head visualize, sense and feel your mind connected to the God source and the spirit world.

Then, as a beginner, total body relaxation is required.

Bring your attention to your feet. Relax

Focus on your lower legs and knees. Relax

Focus on your upper legs. Relax

Focus on your hips, pelvis and buttocks. Relax

Focus on your tummy and lower back

Relax; let your intuition or gut feelings prepare for spirit contact. Ask your guide or doorkeeper to bring on this awareness. If you don't know them just telepathically ask your higher self and recognize that it had been granted

Now bring your attention to your chest, upper back and shoulders. Relax

Focus on your upper arms, lower arms, hands and fingers. Relax

Bring your attention to your throat and neck. Relax

Continue on; focus on your chin, mouth and nose. Relax

Focus on your eyes, ears and forehead. Relax

Focus on the crown of your head. Relax

Now, bring your attention to your third eye, that's located in the center forehead—between both eyes. Prepare your self for spirit contact.

Focus on Chakra # 1, the Base, 'end of the spine; open it gently.

Visualize the color RED and cover yourself with this color

Chakra # 2, the Sacral, over the genitals; open it gently

Visualize the color ORANGE and cover yourself with this color

Chakra # 3, the Solar Plexus, over your abdomen; open it gently

Visualize the color YELLOW and cover yourself with this color

Chakra # 4, the Heart, over your centre chest; open it gently.

Visualize the color GREEN and cover yourself with this color

Chakra # 5, the Throat, over the larynx; open it gently.

Visualize the color BLUE and cover yourself with this color

Chakra # 6, the Brow, center forehead,—the third eye-; open it gently.

Visualize the color INDIGO and cover yourself with this color

Chakra # 7, the Crown, top of the head; open it gently.

Visualize the color BRIGHT WHITE. Cover yourself with this color and totally fill the room with BRIGHT WHITE.

NOW, SPEAK TO YOUR DOORKEEPER GUIDE AND ASK THEM TO KEEP YOU RELAXED AND IN A MEDITATIVE STATE UNTIL YOU SPEAK SPIRITS WORDS (If alone) OR YOUR NAME IS CALLED BY A TEACHER OR YOUR LEADER.

Listen to your higher self through the thought process and speak what is being sent to your brain via telepathic communication.

After you have completed a session always go back over your chakra's and close them as not to leave them open for any uninvited intruders. Very important, always thank God, your guides, doorkeeper and those from the spirit world for protection and assistance.

Chapter Eleven
Ghosts, Spirits, Loved Ones

A Message from Home

When time has past and you're all alone
Think of me in our beautiful home
For once we pass through the veil
Death is sweet but who could tell
A transformation that has taken place
By God's sweet hands and his saving grace
I've travelled to a distant shore
Where loved ones meet and part no more
So come to me in our beautiful home
When you're ready to be, yet not alone.

This is probably the longest chapter in the book. It's to bring on awareness that the spirit lives on after physical death and those on the other side often try to contact. Not always in the way we wish but in a way they're able as it takes a tremendous amount of energy to make such a contact.

The ghostly manifestation occurrences you're about to read will demonstrate that there is more than one dimension of reality. Although some loved ones who have passed will appear before you and terrify you; that's not their intention, most of the time they're coming to you with love and appreciation.

Life does exist after what we call death. There isn't any death; a transformation takes place where there's a change of worlds, nothing more. Your soul is energy and that energy can't be destroyed. At death of the human body this energy starts a new existence, in spirit form in a new dimension. Some call it heaven; others call it God's beautiful realm of creation, the Spirit World.

I know I'm going to be with all my loved ones one day, humans and pets alike, who have passed on before me. On many occasions I feel certain loved ones around, sending love, being non-judgemental and accepting me as I am, the way God put me in this world. They're standing by in my decision making and giving me guidance when I need it.

You too may have experienced such as this and let it go as if it's your mind playing tricks on you. It's real, as real as it gets so don't deny but accept the reality of what your loved ones are trying to impress on your brain. Most of the so called ghosts aren't spooks, they're loved ones trying to make contact through the best means they are able, to let us know they still love us and still would like to be in our company.

Don't be afraid of the ones you love who have passed on, for when they appear to you from the other side it's out of their desire to return to someone such as you, whom they love.

Health Care Institutions

I was new to the City of Toronto in 1983 and had no problem finding work. Being a newcomer, I applied at several areas below my skills, as well as at the standard level recognized and approved by the medical college of Ontario, which I became a part of as soon as my legal papers were in order. I took the first job offered so I could get established. I took a job below my qualifications but remained for only a short period of time. This experience was a positive eye opener but after a term of unhappiness in the environment I chose to move on.

A couple a friends were working at another health care institution in the downtown core. I applied and got a job. There were two supervisors, out of six, with whom you could associate and rely on for guidance and advice. You knew they were caring nurses and when they approached you knew they respected the professional person you are. These two people were a pleasure and they would be greeted with a smile of acceptance when visiting the unit. These wonderful caring loving nurses will forever remain in my heart. We gave great care and usually had a very good non-stressful shift as a group. Those times were happy and we made the best of it. I took this job and stayed for 8 years; A12-hour shift tour gave one more time away from work, so it seemed, but not less hours. This was perfect as younger people like to have more time for social life and this was the perfect scenario.

There was some talk about ghosts appearing on certain floors and doing certain things to the patients and staff etc. Those stories would circulate mostly at nights when all the patients were sleeping and we wanted something exciting to talk about to help us stay awake and to pass away the time.

All such places have legends and this institution was no exception.

I believed in the supernatural and took those ghostly stories to heart and didn't reject anything that I thought was possible. Throughout my life I had similar episodes happening but nothing that I couldn't handle with my own inner feelings.

There's one particular event that happened personally while I was a staff member and I like to share it with you.

There was a kind and dear old Polish woman who had bilateral leg amputations. That means she had both legs removed up to the hip area and was left with two stumps. She couldn't speak English but interpreters for such people as this were close by. In an interview they were hired for that purpose as well as past experiences. Most all languages spoken had an interpreter either on the job or one that could be reached 24 hours a day.

This woman specifically asked for a DNR, which means 'do not resuscitate'. This means that if she died of natural causes she didn't want anyone to do Cardio Pulmonary Resuscitation, CPR. That was written on her chart in large bright red letters and all the staff knew we followed their wishes regarding a choice made by a competent person.

I quickly came to realize that apparitions of the deceased don't always look exactly as they did before they died. Some will appear to you as you remember them, or quite often in certain cases they'll appear younger, healthier and less stressed than when they were on the earth plane.

This dear woman decided it was time to go to the spirit world on a day when I happened to be on duty. I was in her room at the time as well as a Yugoslavian nurse who wasn't registered with the college of Ontario. She was a very good caring nurse but she didn't want to let her die, even though the lady wanted to.

The patient started to gasp for a couple of last breaths and then it ceased. With that, the Yugoslavian nurse yelled at me to call a code, jumped up on the bed, knelt by the patient's side and proceeded to do CPR.

I looked at her and said that she should get off the bed and stop the CPR, and that she should know this woman doesn't want to be resuscitated. She said, "Come on, help me." I said, "No, this woman's wish is to die so let her be. Please respect her wishes." With that she yelled out again, "Help, help." I said, "Go ahead and do the CPR but you'll do it alone, SHE DOESN'T WANT CPR. IT'S ON HER CHART; DIDN'T YOU SEE IT THERE?" I left the room and walked out to the main station. I got the charge person and told her what was going on in that room. She walked down the hall, like a Sergeant Major, went into the room, looked at the nurse and said, "Get off the bed and leave this dear woman alone. There's a no-code ordered so have respect for her wishes and stop what you're doing." With that the nurse got off the bed and the screens were pulled. As we stood by her bedside I held her hand and she slipped peacefully away.

Routine procedures were done and after she was pronounced dead and all legalities met by the attending physician she was left in silence for a while, and then her body was taken to the morgue.

I felt good about the fact that she got her wish and as she was dying, I said telepathically, "Go with God."

About two weeks later I was working, what we called the graveyard shift, night shift. I start at 7 PM and worked until 7 AM. I was entitled to an hour break and I was allowed to spend it in whatever way I wished.

I usually chose to go to an unoccupied private room, or find a quiet little nook to have a short sleep on a stretcher and have someone waken me when the hour was up. This particular night I was given a break at midnight. There was a private room unoccupied and I decided to use it. I told the charge nurse where

I would be so that she would wake me in an hour. She said, "Right-O, have a good nap" and off I went to prepare my bed. I put a clean sheet over the clean ones that were already there, got in bed for a peaceful, badly needed nap and covered myself with a blanket.

I was no sooner lying down and then I felt the door open. There was a little breeze of wind and a slight cold chill went all over my body. I thought it was the charge nurse wanting some information before I went off to sleep. I raised myself up on one elbow, looked to see the door still closed and there was the Polish woman who had died two weeks ago. My heart stood still and the cold chill that went down my back was like something I've never experienced before in my lifetime. This was unexpected as it had been such little time for her in the spirit world. She looked much younger and very healthy. She's now standing there on two beautiful legs and smiling pleasantly down at me. She never spoke but I knew what she was saying to me telepathically. She must have felt my fear because she slowly vanished and I could feel her gratitude for my intervention during her passing. Until this day I can see her so vividly in my mind, I'll never forget the feeling of her thanks towards me.

Needless to say, I got out of bed and went back to the unit station. The night charge nurse said, "Thought you went on break." I said I did and that I didn't feel sleepy and someone else may go if they wish. I chose not to tell them about my visitor at this time or nobody else would have gone for a break that night.

About a week later I told the night staff about my experience, but only after we'd all had our break. There were once again ghost stories told throughout the night when time permitted until it came time to give morning care.

This dear spirit had gotten enough energy to appear to me,

just to let me know that she is happy where she is and also to show me that she was now complete with two legs again. She looked so beautifully young and happier. She looked so much at peace and her smile was enough to show me she was now very contented.

Thank you, dear spirit, for presenting yourself to me even though you startled me nearly half to death. I dealt with it as maturely as I could and finally grasped the meaning behind her apparition.

Greenwood Avenue Rental

I rented a house in the City of Toronto along Danforth Avenue in 1989. It's an old two storey Victorian house with lots of character and charm and I appreciated its location. The basement apartment was finished and was also included in the rental price.

My daughter and my brother also moved in with me. All three bedrooms were upstairs on the second floor, with a one-bedroom apartment in the basement area that we used as a guest room and a den. We hadn't moved in long when I felt another presence about the house. This presence would create the most distracting noises when I was in the shower or when I was doing a cleaning of the lower house on Sunday mornings. Often when I was in the shower I would hear someone walking up the stairs and walking about the floor close to the bathroom door. Many times I would call out to see who had come home unexpectedly. I never got an answer and the walking would stop. It got so loud one day, I heard someone running up the stairs as if there was an emergency. I knew all the doors were locked and that I was definitely alone; so I though! The shower scene at Bates Motel from Alfred Hitchcock's movie 'Psycho' immediately popped into my mind with me as another victim in a similar situation. It was a creepy feeling and cold shivers went down my spine at the thoughts. I got out of the shower, pulled on my robe with water going everywhere and went to investigate.

I called out my daughter's name—no answer. I called out my brother's name—no answer. I checked the doors; all were closed and still locked. I made a thorough investigation of the house only to find I was alone. I went back to finish my shower, no sooner back there when I heard the running up the stairs again and heavy walking about the floor outside the bathroom door. I called out again, no answer. I finished my shower very quickly and got out. I made another total check of the house and found nothing.

I sat down and began thinking. I knew at this point in my life that there was an existence after death and the soul doesn't die along with the body. I sat for a few moments at the top of the stairs and said, "OK, now who are you?" No answer. I asked again and this time I heard a faint voice within myself say, "Miranda." I started to ask her questions but didn't know how to make further contact. I knew I had this ability but didn't know how to put it to proper use at this time.

I told my daughter, my brother and a special friend about this. My brother tried to find a logical explanation and tried to explain how all of this could be created physically. He also thought I was kidding him and when I stood by my word, he thought I had finally lost it. My daughter on the other hand said, "I know she's here, she's in my room a lot." I asked her to explain this and she said she felt a spirit around and felt that this spirit shared her bedroom with her. She also said that this spirit once used the bedroom she is now in and that they both communicated together on several occasions. Now, I thought my daughter was pulling my leg or if she'd finally lost it as had

I, but then I believed every word she said. I told my friend. She always believed my stories about the afterlife and it was always followed by several questions.

As time went on I got used to the walking and running up the stairs and around the floor outside the bathroom. Miranda got bolder and bolder. She would have fun with me and turned off the vacuum cleaner on several occasions. This would annoy me but I accepted her playful behaviour. One day as I was in the kitchen cleaning, I felt her presence very strongly. I would speak to her often now, especially when I was alone.

This time I didn't speak to her but turned around quickly, and then I saw a silhouette of her jump up out of the easy chair and run up the stairs. This explains the running up the stairs.

I told my daughter and friend about this but not my brother.

It seemed like it was only during the day she was active with me but at night she was active with my daughter.

Finally, a time came when my brother was home alone during the day. He had a day off and decided to sleep in awhile. When he awakened he went directly to the shower before going downstairs to have breakfast. He said when he was in there; he heard footsteps coming up the stairs and someone walking around the landing. He said he thought it was one of us home early and didn't pay much attention to it. When he finally investigated he found he was alone and all the doors were closed and locked. He wanted to know if I had come home and left again. I hadn't. I told him it was Miranda; he rolled his eyes, shook his head and went on his way.

Miranda wasn't a bad Ghost; she was a lonely spirit who didn't make the transition well and stayed within the earth plane. I didn't mind her sharing the house with us because I felt a lot of love and comfort coming from her when she was at her peak. She was also a comfort to my daughter and she also felt this affection. Needless to say, Miranda was with us and didn't bother us very much after we recognized her and accepted her as she was. Not sure if she knew she had passed over but she seemed a very contented being as she was and didn't seem to seek answers from us. If she did it wasn't anything of which I was aware.

When we moved I assumed she stayed where she was. I do hope her soul finally moved on with the help of her relatives and loved ones from the other side, and that they finally came and took her home.

New Home Purchased after the Rental

Six years ago I bought a beautiful three-bedroom bungalow that consists of two bathrooms and a finished basement in Scarborough, Ontario, Canada. It was exactly what I was looking for. Most of all, it had a large garden and I couldn't have asked for a better one.

I happily moved in and got settled away.

My first priority was building a new sunroom and a garage. I did that immediately and dearly love the decision. It sets the house off well with this addition and the sunroom became my main room in the house. It overlooks the beautiful garden and I use it summer and winter. It's heated with a gas fireplace during the wintertime, which makes it very comfortable and cozy.

When I moved in I chose my bedroom. I chose the one in between the dining room and the second bedroom. So, I guess I chose the first bedroom you meet while walking down the hallway.

My brother chose the 2nd bedroom and I converted the 3rd bedroom into a library. You have to walk through the library to get to the sunroom.

There's a bedroom and bathroom in the basement area that I use as a guestroom and is also used as a den or an entertainment area.

I felt I've had clairvoyant abilities for a very long time and didn't know how to use my talent or gift correctly, until recently.

I hadn't been here very long when I sensed another spirit about this house as well. I felt his presence more in the basement area, especially in the workroom. The first time I sensed this spirit (*ghost...most people would call it*) was in the darkened area in the basement. I could hear him breathing and I knew he had died with a respiratory disease. I asked his name and he gave it to me.

A few nights later while I was almost asleep, I felt movement in my bed. It felt like someone was walking back and forth on the bed. It would walk half way up from the foot of the bed as far as my tummy and turn around and walk down to my feet and up the other side until it got to my tummy again. Back again etc. etc. It never came any further than that. I first thought the cat got out of the room and was in bed with me. I searched for her but she was in her room downstairs, with the door closed. I went back to bed. Said a prayer for protection and went to sleep.

This walking over the bed went on nightly for a long time. I felt that this restless spirit/ghost didn't want to hurt me or it would have by now, so I accepted that it was there with me. No problem, I've been aware of spirits approximately all throughout my lifetime and kept it mostly to myself, except for one good friend of mine. We all need respect and I was also respecting this ghost because he also deserves it. With it comes a little fear of the unknown and what it might do to me while I'm asleep.

The man had already passed to spirit when I bought the house from his wife and daughter. I never knew his name.

Finally I phoned the daughter to have a little chat. I stepped lightly on the subject and was cautious not to be so blunt with my questions. After a while chatting, I asked her if anything ever happened in the house, like someone died in there.

She said no, not that she was aware of. She said her dad died in the hospital shortly after they took him there. I asked if her dad had a breathing problem and used a humidifier. She said yes, he was asthmatic and had a touch of emphysema. He used it all the time. I then asked if there was anything strange that happened in the first bedroom. She said, "No but my father was placed in that room in the last year of his life, but didn't die in there." I thought that explains who's in my room with me.

I went on talking about the events that had been happening to me since I moved in and what I sensed around me. She confirmed that her father's name was the one that I was given and that he dearly loved his house. He was a good man and wouldn't hurt anyone. He spent a lot of time in his workroom in the basement because he was a bit of a handyman.

The walking over my bed continued. I started to talk to him. I started to tell him that this is my house now and reminded him that he was dead; he should look for the light and follow it. I don't think he believed it and that upset him because he got a little meaner to me during the night. He now would walk all over the bed, not just the lower half. His respect for me seems to have vanished. One night he pressed down on my head so hard, I had to get angry and yelled at him to get off. He listened and let me go.

The next night my feet were hanging over the foot of the bed, uncovered. An excruciating pain awakened me. It felt like someone had scraped a sharp nail down the centre of my right foot. I woke up in so much pain; I started cussing at him and told him to leave me alone. He did. He'd had his fun for the night, and let me sleep the rest of it.

He scraped my foot twice more, at two different times, during that month. He was now determined to get me out of his room, maybe his house.

I'm not a raised Roman Catholic but someone suggested that I use some Holy Water. She actually provided it and said that she got it from the Roman Catholic Church and I blessed my room and the whole house. What did I have to lose; at this point in my frustration I'd try anything. From then on I said protection prayers daily and he seemed to leave me alone for a while. Maybe the prayers alone would have done it, but nevertheless! I was satisfied with the results.

Finally he got restless again. About two years ago, during the night, he walked all over my bed again. I ignored him this time, mumbled a prayer and then he had the nerve to scrape my foot again. This time it hurt more than any other time. This mean ghost was getting more violent and seemed to want me out of his home, which is now legally mine. This was 3 o'clock in the morning and I had to get up to go to a 12-hour workday at 5 AM. I finally cracked. I sat up in bed and started cussing at him again, saying cuss words more times than I can remember. Enough is enough. During this cussing, he went underneath the bed and gave 4 violent heavy kicks making the mattress move. He was not happy with me one bit. Now, for the first time I'm a little scared. I got out of bed, got the Holy Water, showered my bed room, asked God for protection and help, and then went to the den in the basement to sleep for the remaining time. I told this spirit/ghost to go to the light and look for God because he's now dead and the house legally belongs to me. Leave right now. He settled down again. He hasn't gotten that bad since, but he's still here.

My brother is very skeptical and doesn't believe in spirits or ghosts. I used to tell him about this, he would listen but I knew he thought I was losing it and finally going crazy.

My Mother, plus other people would visit me from time to time. I would give up my bedroom to them while they were here and I would use the one in the basement area.

My Mother never felt anything while she was in my room. For one thing, she was very spiritual and religious. She prayed faithfully every night. God protected her and maybe my spirit/ghost liked a woman sleeping there and not me. All my guests in that room were women and not one was bothered by him, making me look as crazy as my brother was thinking I was.

One night while my Mother was here and I slept in the basement bedroom, something unusual did happen. That morning my brother sat down and had breakfast with us. He asked why did I get up during the night and go to the sunroom to rock in the rocking chair, keeping him awake. This chair has a little squeak when it is rocked back and forth.

I told him that I didn't wake all night and had one of my most restful sleeps in a long time. He asked my Mother if she went there and she said she hadn't. She also slept very well. I told him it was our spirit/ghost and he'd seen a woman in my bed and needed a place to stay. My spirit/ghost was the one rocking in the chair! He thought I was joking with him again. I was totally serious. I do believe it was our ghost; no one else was here but us three, plus our ghost.

The second night, the same thing happened. He told my mom and me about the rocking of the chair during the night. I asked if he got up to check on it, he said he hadn't. I felt he was a little scared and frightened to investigate; maybe a fear of finding out what was really causing the rocking. I would have gotten up and had a talk with the old devil. I think my brother finally began to believe what I had been trying to tell him all along.

Little over a year ago my sister was visiting. She stayed in the bedroom down in the den. It was summer and the basement area is cooler and she liked the coolness. One night while she was sleeping, she felt someone rubbing his hand down over her head as if they were caressing her with affection. Her first reaction was that it was I because I'm very fond of this particular sister. When she opened her eyes to see me, she saw nothing and got a little scared. She told me of this event the next day and that she almost came and got in bed with me. I asked her about what took place and how she sensed things. She said she was afraid but got a sense of love and peace from it. She said she relaxed herself after a while and drifted back to sleep. When she did finally tell me about it, I told her of my spirit/ghost and if he caressed her head, he obviously liked her, where as he didn't like me that much. She didn't know of my extra guest, spirit/ghost…and said, "Oh My God, if I knew you had a ghost I wouldn't have slept down there alone."

I proceeded to tell her of all the things that had happened to me since I moved into this house. She was a little nervous but I calmed her down. I told her that he's actually a nice ghost once we cleared the air and he has been leaving me alone for some time now.

About eight months ago, I was sitting and talking on the phone with a friend of mine. I was alone but glanced to my left only to see my spirit/ghost lying on the couch in the living room, as if he was taking a nap. I feel he was watching TV. I only saw from his feet up to his chest. I didn't see his face because there's a corner wall that was blocking my view. I shook my head twice but the image stayed. I saw the clothes he was wearing and still could describe them with ease. It started to fade when I went to look at his face. I immediately spoke to him. I said, (Called him by name). "You know this house is now legally mine. You're very welcome to stay and share it, BUT…YOU GOT TO LEAVE ME ALONE." He faded out of focus and hasn't bothered me since that time.

I feel and see him here often. I sometimes can't find something, I'll ask him where I can find it and he's told me on three or four occasions where I could find what I was looking for. I got a little excited about his accuracy, so I haven't asked him lately, but will probably call on him again if I need his assistance.

My spirit/ghost has settled down tremendously but I never trust him completely. I now know his power beyond the grave and I was told by an experienced medium that he is out of control and needs to be dealt with. She said that I'm much stronger then he is because I have the power of God behind me, so therefore if he continues his negative haunting he well need to be exorcised. I don't want to take him on like that again knowing and experiencing his past behaviour. I feel we finally became friends and he has accepted sharing the house with me.

Thank God.

A Father's Concern Beyond the Grave

A young man separated from his wife about nine months ago. It was his decision and having a new girl friend prior to this was a shock to the whole family. His wife and their two children moved out and went to live in the next town; about 45 minutes drive away from him.

The day his wife and children moved out is the day his new girl friend moved in. That move upset the entire family, except me. I understood the logic behind it because I went through something very similar when I was 25 years old and know only too well what he's going through.

One morning this new girl friend was still in bed and the young man had gone to work. Her sleep was disturbed by something rustling in the room. Then she felt a hand touch her leg to bring her out of her drowsy sleep. When she opened her eyes there was a small man sitting on the foot of the bed looking at her. This young mans father was a small man and she sensed that it was he, although she had never met him. She got very nervous, got out of bed and went to the kitchen. The phone rang and when she answered it her sister was on the other end. She told her sister all about what was going on and hung up. She then went back into the bedroom. Upon her return she was shocked to see him still sitting on the bed. With that she turned around, went out to the phone and called the young man, her boy friend, to tell him about the apparition and ask for his assistance. This young man couldn't do much other than tell her not to be afraid and he probably thought she was also seeing things, as we seldom think of others, unless it's directly in front of us personally. Most people would have fled the scene by now but the young woman had a strong nerve. She hung up the phone and went back into the bedroom, cautiously entered and searched the room. He had left but not without getting a message across to her. She noticed he had knocked over a recent photograph that was there of the young man and of her, his new girlfriend, frightening her all the more. She didn't know what else to do. Her family lives about an hour's drive from her and that's not consoling in her time of need. She knew it wasn't any good to run to the young man's sister next door because they've avoided her from day one. She was alone except for the ghost with no one to turn to.

Like I said, she had nerve and wasn't going to be frightened away by any ghost. Now more than fully awake and the adrenaline running quickly through her body, she decided to leave the bedroom again and return to the living room.

The young man is a very good carpenter and designer. He

designed and made an oak headstone for his father's grave. This he has completed and had it in his living room awaiting everyone's approval before placing it at the gravesite.

When this new girlfriend went back to the living room this head stone was moved and turned upside down. This scared her half to death. She again phoned the young man at his work.

This young man and his father had a very special bond. If anyone followed in his father's footsteps, it was he. They were very compassionate, caring and loving men. They both love to fish and hunt. They both were very good carpenters and great with children, always doing well for others and helping in any way possible.

His father is more than aware of what's going on, although he's now in spirit. He loved his son's wife like another daughter. He helped his son build his house when they decided to get married. His father dearly loved his youngest grand daughter, who is now 15 years old.

I assume that when his father came to visit he had noticed all that had taken place since his departure. He couldn't bear the fact that his little grand-daughter, whom he loved so dearly, his son's wife, and their oldest daughter, who is now 18 years old, had been replaced by another younger woman who is only 19 years of age. By doing all of this, it's his way of expressing himself and getting a message to his son letting him know of his disapproval. His father was a man who minded his own business, even when it came to his own children. He would let his sons and daughters make their own mistakes and learn from them, but may God help you if anyone tried to hurt any of his family. He would be heard in a way that was very loud through his actions and yet quiet words. He considered his son's wife as another daughter because she was only 18 years old when they married and moved in the house next door to him. He's obviously not approving of this situation and knows that his son is suffering too, as well as his wife and children. He came to try and send the other woman away because he knows there has been a big mistake made and it's still time to make it right.

This young man remains in contact with his wife and children, although his new girl friend doesn't approve of it. They continue to talk and they both feel there's a possibility of a reunion in the future, when all is said and done.

At the present time the new girl friend still remains there, possibly until this young man's father's spirit makes another appearance or sends someone else in his place to try and set things right concerning the break-up of his most cherished son and his family. I had a chance to speak with her just recently and asked her if this spirit had spoken to her. She said yes he did. I asked her what he had to say. She said that he said, "Get out; you'll never have any peace while you're in this house." She paid no mind to what he said. It's been a year now and she's still there but there are strange things happening to her that she says is not from the results of the ghost but from her own accidents and falls. Who's to say she's being honest about this but just a matter of speaking, to remain there without others involvement.

Stories from a Very Reliable Source, My Mother

Hopefully those stories will leave you with an abiding certainty that what we call death; is not the end of life. I believe the subject will see what they need to see at a specific moment, when the time has come for reassurance and proof.

My Dad died April 15, 1998. He suffered from a stroke at age 64 and had a few mild strokes as he progressed on in years.

None of them were severe enough to kill him but it disabled him little by little at each occurrence. When he became unable to care for himself my mother had to take an early retirement in order to care for him. This went on for a number of years until it came that she needed help in his daily care. She eventually got a couple of caregivers to assist her. This also gave her a chance to get out and do her errands etc. and get back into her long lost routine way of life. She had great support from her family when she needed it and I took my vacation time to be with him during three of his hospital stays. I'm still very thankful to have spent this time with him, even though I was his private nurse at the time, even though it was in a hospital room.

A short while after my dad's body was put to rest, my mom heard from an old friend of hers. He's a second cousin and a younger man by 20 years than my mom. He phoned her out of the blue after years of no contact, to say that his wife had taken ill with undetected cancer. He said now it has metastasised to her vital organs and was rapidly spreading over her entire body.

He said he needed to express himself and that my mother was the first to come into his mind when he was thinking of reaching out to someone. He also said he was made aware of her from a source he couldn't explain and he needed to talk to her about his wife and her prognoses.

Mostly he made nightly phone calls. My mother listened to his sadness and sympathized with him. He told her about this one particular night while he was sitting by his dying wife holding her hand. He said she looked up at him and said, "The room is full of Angels, don't you see them?" He said, "No honey, I don't see them but if you see them, they're really here."

This dying woman knew how her husband was hurting and she tried to hang on to life as long as she could, on his behalf. Then one afternoon while he was sitting by her bedside once again, holding her hand, she looked up at him for the last time and said, "My Angels are back and they want me to go with them." He knew she was holding on to life for the one and only reason, him. He looked at her, smiled and said, "Honey its ok; you may go with your Angels."

He held her in his arms; she closed her eyes and went with her Angels, who were so patiently waiting to take her home, to her loved ones on the other side.

Before my mother could make arrangements to go to the city, his wife passed away very quickly and had left him devastated. Her dying so young and so suddenly was way beyond his understanding; he suffered in silence.

My mother went to see him at the funeral and tried in her own caring way to console him, even though she was dealing with her own loss, my dad.

This consoling went on for about six months and my mother felt she wasn't getting anywhere with him and his grieving. She stayed with him for up to a week at a time so they both had each other and someone else who could relate to what they were both experiencing. She listened to his sadness, shared his stressful anxiety and knew it was affecting his mental and general health. She strived to bring him into a positive frame of mind and tried to get him as relaxed as possible. I give my mother a ten for all her many moments of listening to him and reaching out with her words of comfort.

My mother had accepted the passing of my father well. He had a long illness and she was expecting his passing at any time. This may lessen the pain a little but the pain of losing someone you love is still there, nonetheless.

Her friend was going through a very rough time considering the sudden loss of his young wife. He grieved himself into a depression and it was taking its toll on my mother. She remained with him as much as she could and encouraged him to have a closer contact with his children and his granddaughter. She knew that an emotional trauma like this has got to be the hardest for anyone to deal with.

He finally took her advice and started to have his granddaughter there on the weekends my mother was there.

About six months after the passing of his wife, he decided to go to the gravesite, taking my mother and his five-year-old granddaughter. As they were standing there, he was still grieving and was still very angry about losing his dearly beloved wife. They were speaking in hushed tones when suddenly his granddaughter became very excited, pointed above the grave and shouted out, "Look grandpa, there's grandma." He asked where and she pointed again and said, "There," pointing in the same direction. She said, "She's standing there and smiling at us." My mother said, "Sure she is darling, give her our love." With that she watched her grandma slowly vanish. This left my mother and her friend in awe, as it confirmed that there is an existence after the grave. He gradually improved after this occurrence and my mother eased herself away once she noticed he was coping well.

Today, a couple of years later, she tells me he's now gotten on with his life and has met a lady friend, who is more than just a friend.

Five years later this man also went to spirit. He didn't cope as well as we had thought and had always grieved silently. Now he's happily with his wife once more.

It's amazing the power of our young children's minds. They are much more capable of seeing our spirit friends and relatives clairvoyantly than most adults see.

Studies have shown that there are more than 50% of widows who have experienced apparitions of a departed husband more so than any other. Can you imagine what the percentage of children who have seen an apparition and were told, there's nothing there, and it's your imagination. In such a case as this try to be more understanding of the child, even ask the child to talk to the apparition. Try to get him or her to ask short questions and see what information that will get from the world behind the veil.

An Acquaintance from My High School Days

Death itself is beautiful. There's a great feeling of peace and it's more pleasant than life itself. I'm sure the family of this young man is wondering what the purpose of life is; and what would be the purpose of losing a young husband, and a caring father.

Once again I'll tell you the story as my mother has told me.

This man and I went to high school together. He was a couple of years younger and a couple of grades behind me. We knew each other, liked each other, and recognized each other but we weren't close friends. When we left high school we both went our separate ways. I moved to the city, he stayed in our little town, got married and settled down. He was a good husband and a good provider for his wife and children. He stayed fairly active in sports whereas I had given that up a long time ago. Small towns are like that. Everyone knows what the other person is doing and some of them make it their business as well.

One day while he was playing soccer with his usual team he got a swift kick in the lower leg, leaving quite a large bruise. I don't know what a man in his late forties was doing at this sport anyway. He couldn't continue with the game due to the severe pain. During the late evening he had to make a visit to the local emergency. He was given a medication for pain and told to go home and rest. He did this but had one of the worst nights of his life. He remained in pain even though he took a strong analgesic. The next day about noon he couldn't take it anymore. He asked his wife to drive him back to the emergency. They got ready and while he was just about to get into the car, he said, "I'm dying". His wife said, "No you're not, don't be so foolish." He said, "Yes I am." She said, "Why do you say something like that?" He said, "Because all I see are bright lights and hear beautiful music." Within a few seconds this man's body was lying on the ground and his wife panicking with fear. She yelled for help and the ambulance was called. This man was dead when the paramedic attendant arrived. He was rushed to the local hospital nonetheless. The attending doctor pronounced him DOA, Dead On Arrival.

Because of his questionable death, by law there has to be an autopsy. They found that this young man had a clot that dislodged in his leg and made its way to his brain causing an aneurysm, and then finally death occurred. A physician did not detect this because he probably thought a young man wouldn't have to worry about something of this nature.

We all have some sense or a form of seeing our guardian angels. There's always some way of knowing, "Hey, it's my turn and I'm now well aware of it." No matter how one perceives it to be, there's always a warm feeling of inner peace and an acceptance of what's about to occur. During the final moments of transition, there will be a warm loving presence of God. Your guardian Angels will assist and guide you. Progressing onward to that beautiful place of the spirit world where we're all welcomed with a wonderful feeling of love from souls we've always known.

Chapter Twelve
Private Readings

Reaching out to Spirit

Your visits were short but so intense
Your light a burning flame
You came to me from across the veil
And gave me your true name
You came to say you're at peace now
When called upon how you came
To comfort and apologize to the heart that cared
For silently she mourned her loss for years
God Bless you. Be at peace.

One of the greatest rewards of making contact with Spirit is being in a crowd of people giving messages and a loved one comes through who is immediately recognized. It's also a good feeling when the person or persons involved come to you after the service to let you know that they are pleased with their messages. Sometimes they ask questions about what else I may have picked up when I probably had cut the message short so that I could go to the next person who also had a loved one waiting to come through. I'll tell them what else there is but sometimes it's as long as a week or more before they approach me. Because it's been that long, I may have to ask them to refresh my memory as to what was brought forward and given, as I don't always remember all that I give. When they tell me what was given, some of their contacts will return at the same time and give them what they need to hear. On the other hand a small percentage doesn't.

An example of this is when I gave a message to a gentleman that involved a passed loved one. A woman spirit came with so much love and admiration for him, giving me a hug saying that this is for him and also telling him that she was pleased that the wheel chair was not being used anymore. I had no idea what all of this was about and told him that. I hoped he understood because right now that's all she's giving me and I don't understand the significance behind it. This message had not left my mind and it bothered me because it was such a strong motherly vibration of love and I was almost certain it was his mother.

The next time I saw this man was two weeks later and he just happened to sit behind me at a church gathering. The service hadn't started so I asked him about the message and if it had made any sense to him. He said that he had meant to tell me about it because it was his aunt who came through. She had never married because she was in a wheelchair and considered him to be one of her children; treating him as a son she never had as she did with some of her other nieces and nephews.

I don't usually approach someone about a message but when such a strong vibration as this comes through it makes me curious as to whom that spirit may be and what was meant by such a message. His verification gave me contentment because his aunt is very happy on the other side. She presented herself on a beach giving a very elaborate, organized and peaceful party.

Here's another story for those of you who'd like to read about one of my first private readings. I don't do private reading as a rule but have taken the odd one or two, with no charge. I have permission from Mrs. Zee to use it.

I knew very little about this woman's past and that I never got interested enough to pry into it either. God directed our friendship from a mutual friend whom got us together.

Mrs. Zee has been a dear friend of mine for many years. She phoned me one day and said, "My ex-husband had died two years ago and I just found out about it." I knew there was an ex-husband and that was the extent of it. She never volunteered any information and it wasn't my business to inquire. Why freshen and open old wounds? She also said she would like to make contact with his spirit if it was at all possible.

I told her not to tell me anything about him now, especially his name as if I could get him to tell it to me it would verify my contact with his spirit. I told her that I'd get my meditation friend and development partner Bonnie to sit with us and we'll see what comes through, if anything. I got in touch with my friend and she said she'd be more then happy to participate.

As time went on Mrs. Zee got a little restless waiting for all three of us to get together. One day she visited and asked if I would try to make contact alone, as it would be some time before Bonnie could make it. I'd never done this in the company of only one person as I prefer other witnesses; I usually do this in the company of two or more. I said we could try if she'd like but maybe I won't get anything. This satisfied her but then again she's had confidence in me for years.

We made ourselves comfortable.

I told Mrs. Zee to focus on her contact and will his spirit to come.

I put on a New Age Musical CD and sat in a comfortable chair with my hands laid on my upper legs, palms up, while Mrs. Zee sat directly across from me. I said a protection prayer that went something like this. *Holy Great Spirit, please give us your protection, surround us with your White Light and bring forth the spirit that we so would like to make contact with. Amen.*

As the music played we both concentrated on clearing our minds of everyday matters to listen to what spirit has to bring forth into our senses. I could feel Mrs. Zee's energy reaching out and calling for her ex-husband to make an appearance.

We sat for about 5 minutes when I saw two white lights traveling towards me. One was much brighter than the other. When I felt their vibrations I spoke to Mrs. Zee and asked if I may speak to her. I knew those two contacts were for her as she's the only person there. The two lights finally arrived and this is how the contact goes as far as I remember it.

The bright light entity spoke and said, "I'm Steve, she knows who I am, and I have Alber, Albrit, Albrig, with me." (I couldn't quite make out the name properly although he tried a couple of times) This name didn't sound complete to me but I pronounced it as I heard it. He was telepathically giving me this and he spoke very fast, so therefore I couldn't catch it.

Steve said, "We are friends now; I'm here to talk for him because he's not strong and unable to communicate on his own."

When I mention the word 'he', the entity is referring to Steve and he's the one doing the talking...

He began to speak and I told Mrs. Zee all that I could catch as speaking was very quickly. He said, "*the only unfinished business there is, is that there's a document in a safety deposit box that you would probably be interested in, but if it's never revealed you won't lose a great deal but it's of interest to you. There was some communication later in life when you got back in contact with each other. There was an exchange of letters, cards and postcards for a period of time and you've kept some of them. He said to go look for them, especially the first two you received and reread them. You need to read between the lines: because you have missed a message that was there for you.*" He also said "*my mother wasn't a very good influence when I was younger and I'm sorry for that.*"

While in this semi trance state my arms and chest muscles became very tight. I felt the spirit of her ex-husband entering my body. He began to communicate with me now, he said the tightening I could feel in my arms and chest is him holding Mrs. Zee. He said to tell her he's hugging her. I gave her this message but he kept holding on until he almost exhausted me. I asked him to leave but he wouldn't let go. I got firm with him and told him to leave again; then I saw the duller light disappear in the distance.

Steve stayed behind, he's not finished yet. He said he had lots of experience at this and he's strong. He wanted to tell Mrs. Zee, Thank You, for getting involved with the documentation done on him since his passing. He really respects her for this. He also said, "*I have something for you to tell my wife, your sister. I love her very much and I adore her. Tell her when she has the next pain in her right shoulder blade in her back that will be an indication that I'm around and please talk to me.*"

I watched as the bright white light of Steve went out of focus. I came back from my semi trance. I felt totally wiped and needed a rest.

Mrs. Zee was pleased with her reading.

We didn't talk a lot after the reading as we had to get on with our day, but Mrs. Zee took the time to reply and verify the message with a written thank you.

Mrs. Zee's Reply:

Hello: The only thing you missed out is that you got his name, even though it didn't sound like a real name to you. I met him as 'Brig' but his real name was Alastair. So when you hit 'Albrig' you got it right, even though it didn't make sense to you. You actually got it the very first time—the other attempts came when that one didn't make sense. I think I've shredded all cards from him just about two months before I moved, not sure if there's any more around. You were absolutely right about his mother!

Love Mrs. Zee.

This reading wasn't enough for Mrs. Zee. She wanted more! I'm not sure why she wanted to make this contact after so many years of being apart. But she asked if I would sit with her once again. I said yes, what are friends for, but this time my friend Bonnie has to be there. This was good for her, as she'll have the two of us making contact for her with any luck.

Mrs. Zee's 2nd Reading:

Mrs. Zee came by on Wednesday evening. Shortly after that Bonnie arrived. We chatted for a while and than proceeded to the living room. I turned on the red light and dimmed the ceiling lights. I presented them both with a large silk yellow sunflower, as a close divine connection and to help bring awareness of Spirit and then I put on some soft New Age music. We got comfortable and sat in our awareness position, as we do to meditate.

I said a protection Prayer. It went something like this.

Great Divine Spirit. Please protect us with your White Light while we go deep within ourselves and communicate with our spirit contact. Bring him forward with inspiring words and wisdom for our friend Mrs. Zee. Amen.

I continued to talk. I talked a meditation, similar to number two in the back of the book. At the end of it I also included; Now…Within your peaceful mind, take one last look at the far end of the meadow. You'll see a dim light coming towards you. As it's getting closer, you'll notice it's taking the shape of a man. This man is the spirit we want to communicate with, quietly speak to him, listen to his story so we can relay all messages he will freely give.

I sat quietly and envisioned the scene I just described; it didn't take long for him to make contact as he had been waiting.

This Is What I Received

I saw a light come towards me and as it got brighter I saw another one come in the distance, but it stayed at the back of the meadow. As this spirit got close enough, we began conversing.

I said, "Hello; you look a little better and stronger this time."
He said, "Yes I am."
I said, "Mrs. Zee is here to communicate with you."
He said, "Yes, I can see that."
I asked him who the light was in the background, he said, "That's my friend."
I asked if he had anything to say to Mrs. Zee. There was dead silence.
I spoke again and said, "She would like some contact with you."

He said, "Yes." Then remained silent.

I asked if I had to ask questions or was he going to volunteer.

He actually appeared to be lost for words and he didn't seem to want to volunteer anything.

I asked if he had anything to say to her and if he would like to give her some insight into what went on and what's going on.

He said. "What does she want to know?"

I felt the other light moving closer now. I told the other spirit that I wanted to interact with my first contact. I then asked my contact if this was agreeable with him and if he was strong enough and that I wouldn't deplete him completely.

He said, "That's my friend Steve."

I said, "Steve, please stay away and let me speak with Alastair;" He quickly reminded me that his name is Brig.

I said, "Sorry. Brig."

I told him to direct his energy to Mrs. Zee and have her send me a telepathic message of what she wanted to know.

I waited for a short time and felt Mrs. Zee's energy enter my vibration. There was only one word from her. Everything.

I told him, "Everything."

He said, "I heard." Then continued, "Tell her I'm so sorry for all that has happened, but it's a little late for this, isn't it? I need her forgiveness. My mother was a very strong woman and she—Mrs. Zee—wasn't strong enough to combat her. My mother beat me real bad one time when I got drunk." (He presented himself as a high school student drinking with his buddies. He said he did this frequently because he loved the taste of it and was his way of dealing with his mother's strong parenting.) "Tell her, I'll stay by her side and look over her left shoulder, as her right one is being occupied at the moment. Tell her I need her permission to do that. I cannot just do it without her granting it." He also said, "I'll be patiently waiting for her to guide her safely along, when her time of transition comes."

Mrs. Zee gave him her forgiveness and her permission.

I watched as the two lights gradually disappeared. Then Bonnie and I gave Mrs. Zee the information we received.

This Is What Bonnie Received

I saw a silhouette of a gentleman coming out of the light. He shook hands with me and gave me a sunflower. It was so vivid I almost opened my eyes to see if my flower was still on the table. We were in a wooded area with trees and a river running through it. It was very green, very beautiful. It smelled of nature. There was also a dim light in the background and I wasn't sure what that was.

I had a vision of a boat. He had a fishing rod and began fishing in the river. The stones on the bottom of the river were smooth from the water running over them. The gentleman said he has found peace within himself. He is happy. His time on earth was what it was…Cannot be changed. He turns his back on his past and now goes forward to the light with joy and love. He has learned much but has much more to learn. I saw a stained glass window shaped like a church window, a tall rectangle shape with a rounded top. He has found the path to divine peace, love and joy.

I asked him if he had a message for Mrs. Zee. Out of his cupped hands came a beautiful white dove. He threw it up into the air. He brings peace and love to you Mrs. Zee. He waits patiently for the time when you can be together; for that is one thing he has learned…patience. You won't be together anytime soon…but he will wait patiently. There's a space for you beside him. He'll help you when you pass over but that's not for some time yet.

My next vision came and I saw Joe come toward us. Our

spirit contact, (your Ex-husband), My Spirit Guide and I...Then you Mrs. Zee came into the picture. We all joined to form a circle and said a prayer together. A crystal star came down around this gentleman spirit and than he proceeded toward the light. In his place, a bouquet of calla lilies came out of the earth.

I watched as the two lights disappeared in the distance. I was left with a feeling of great love, coming from him, for you Mrs. Zee.

Mrs. Zee was very pleased and grateful. She said her sister had minor surgery on her back recently exactly where I said she would feel the pain; she'd relay the message to her.

We had a conversation about him and I finally heard of the man she married. I felt it was a big burden lifted of her shoulders when she was finished. His mother was a very controlling woman and still controlled him long after they were married. He had a very bad drinking problem and that was one of the reasons for the divorce. They had a cottage on the lake and he used to fish in the river that Bonnie was shown. The controlling by his mother got so bad that it lead to drinking more alcohol. The problems escalated, leading to a separation and finally divorce.

Chapter Thirteen
Meditation Explained

A Meditation Affirmation

Spirit, flow and release all my fears
Use me to channel your love and peace
Fill me with your power and make me strong
Make me a receptor of your divine intelligence
Heal me and let myself be renewed
Express my perfection, as I remain loyal to you
Fill me with your love, so I may also give love in return
Fill me with devotion, so I may live for thee.
(Some words used are of inspiration from a spiritualist song.)

You didn't buy this book just to read the contents; you bought it to enhance your psychic ability to a point where you'll actually see clairvoyantly. It takes hard 'mental' work, and only with consistent and diligent practise will you achieve it.

The basics are; it's good to have a reliable friend to sit with and learn together. If you don't have one that's interested then try to find a practising group or ask around and find a compatible person, one that has similar interest. Good luck.

There are four meditations involved. They'll give you a direction on where your ability and learning will take you. Hopefully it will give you an incentive to record them for your own personal use. It may be difficult to get used to your own voice, as you'll be listening for errors, punctuation, and grammar mistakes. I suggest that you ask a friend to record them—speaking clearly, accurately and at a slow steady pace. Recording this should be easy as today's modern technology provides an easy means. Purchase a small water fountain and sit it close to the microphone, letting it run while speaking, as a background noise. This will keep your mind focused rather then wander in the wrong direction.

If you're a beginner please do your Inner Relaxation Meditation once a day if time provides and no less then twice a week, if not daily, until you're comfortable with the results before moving on to number two. It's so important that you know how to relax and quiet your mind prior to moving on. The soul purpose of number one is to get you used to keeping your mind focused on nothingness. After a hard stressful day this meditation can also be very responsive to total mind and body relaxation. Number one will bring you from total exhaustion to feeling energized as you let your mind wander on nothingness and your total body will replenish. Repeating this meditation will enable you to keep a clear mind for that amazing contact with spirit in number two.

The more often you do this meditation the more beneficial it is for you in learning the calming technique and quieting your thoughts. Two to three weeks are recommended before moving ahead.

Number two is a visualization meditation; this is the one that will make you clairvoyant, clairaudient and clairsentient with much practise and believing in your self.

Number three is the one where you'll meet your Guardian and number four is to meet your Spirit Guide.

Once you've accomplished all four, create and use one that is appropriate for you, one that's considerably shorter and making it shorter as you progress. As time goes on and you're able to go within quickly, meditation will become very easy. Eventually you'll find you won't need to stack messages and spirit contact will come to you as soon as you call on your spirit guide and focus on whom you would like to give a message to. All good mediums started out stacking messages in meditation whether they agree with me or not, I personally feel that they had.

Please don't go through all the meditations at once, as you'll lose the effects when you do decide to take it more seriously. Follow each meditation to learn how to develop and become clairvoyant through this easy process that I couldn't find anywhere when I was searching. Once you achieve and become aware of an altered state of consciousness your progress will come quickly.

Have you ever been in a crowd of people and had them totally blocked out then someone touches you or mentions your name to bring your attention back to reality? Well, that's very similar to what it feels like in a deep meditation. When this happens you're in a mini state of altered consciousness. If you're aware of it's happening, the next time bring your attention to what's actually being said. Pay close attention to what's going through your mind at that time and you'll be pleasantly surprised of what you'll learn from spirit. Your guides are always with you, they are called guides because that's what they do; they guide and teach you. Once you become aware of them you'll also learn to trust and rely on them more frequently.

Find a church that has a good development circle and join if you can. The good teaching classes fill up fast but strive to get in the one you feel is best. You'll gain extra knowledge from the teacher and many students; you'll also get hands on experience in a group setting. Being among the many students will open your mind quickly to a more creative thinking but you'll be a step ahead of your class and a more advanced student if you follow the guidelines in this book.

If you're an avid meditator you may only need to listen once to number one. Then proceed on to number two in the same session, if you wish. (I say listen because you'll get a much better result and progress a lot faster if you have someone record them on a tape or disc for you).

Stick with the program. Learn how to go within, attune with spirit, develop your abilities, make contact and become clairvoyant. You'll be overwhelmed with the results.

I usually meditate before I retire, at the end of the day. One night before I went to bed I lay down instead of sitting to meditate. I was reasonably new to this but I learned quickly on how to clear my mind and listen to spirit. I was a little sleepy but I was in control. I lay silently and went within. It wasn't long before I was at peace and my mind clear. I was well within and probably on the brink of sleep when I heard a voice say, **"I can help you"**. I was jarred to my senses and spoke out loud and said, **"How?"** Then, I felt the contact fade away. I realized I spoke out loud and had to go back within to connect again. Once I did spirit returned and said again, **"I can help you"**. I spoke telepathically and said, **"Who are you?"** Spirit said, **"Dorcus"**. At that moment I realized I'd forgotten to say my protection prayer prior to meditating. I ignored this contact and said a prayer asking God to watch over me and to protect me, keeping all evil spirits away. I went back to my meditation and listened. Spirit said, **"I didn't like that"**. I asked, **"Are you from God? Are you evil?"** Wrong questions I guess because she became silent. She left and has never returned.

I asked my mother if she knew a Dorcus in the family. She said, *"Yes, she's an aunt by marriage who died when you were very young. She was a good woman who attended church regularly."* She said she felt that she was a good soul.

I can only assume my aunt by marriage came to give me guidance on how to make spirit contact and I upset her by asking or assuming she was an evil entity. She obviously didn't like that assumption and chose not to offer me her assistance again.

"Dear aunt, if I have wounded your beautiful spirit in any way, please forgive me. As I understand from the knowledge my mom has of you, I assume you're a beautiful spirit directed by God. Feel free to communicate with me again and I won't be so apprehensive."

Regardless of any teacher saying a protection prayer in each meditation, it's wise for you to say one all your very own, silently, when you first sit in your chair. Protection is everything and when you protect yourselves with the Beautiful White Light of God no harm will ever come to you. Say your prayer, ask God for protection and visualize yourself surrounded by a white covering as if you were inside a glowing light-filled egg. Jesus said in The Holy Bible in the book of Matthew 6:22. *"Thy whole body shall be full of light."*

Go ahead, say it, and never forget it and remember, we all make contact with the spirit world a little differently, so don't doubt yourself but recognize it when you do. Believe and have confidence in yourself because you already have a psychic gift and this will enhance you to be clairvoyant.

No. 1: Inner Relaxation Meditation

Sit in a comfortable chair or lie comfortably if you're unable to sit. Be aware and try not to fall asleep.

Place your open hands on your upper legs with the palms facing up. (If you're lying down rest them at your sides with the palms facing up, if possible.)

Shift slightly and make sure you're as comfortable as possible; you'll be in this position for about 25 minutes.

(Prayer)

> *Great Divine Spirit. We're aware of your wonderful powers and abilities. Thank you for being here at this time. Please give us protection while we sit in Your presence. Bring our guides through to be by our side while we go within. Make us aware of our guides and gain knowledge from them when the time arises for us to do so. Protect us with your white light and lead us into our higher selves so we'll be in silence with your infinite spirit. Amen*

Close your eyes and listen closely.

Visualize a white beam of light coming through the ceiling. *(Don't let it travel further then my command.)* It's descending upon you. It touches and covers your head and you feel a sense of peace and love from God.

Feel the blissful comfort emitting from it.

It's slowly moving down around your shoulders. It's now covering your arms, your chest and back, your torso and down over your hands. It's moving down around your hips, upper legs, your knees, and your lower legs and slowly moving down around your feet. It's now covering your feet.

Now, visualize it going through the floor underneath you and going deep into mother earth.

You're now grounded and also connected to God.

Don't be afraid, relax, you're safe.

Take in a deep breath. Feel your feet relaxing.

(Let it out slowly as you normally would breath)

(Give time between each for relaxation)

Normal breathe in and feel your lower legs relaxing.

Let it out slowly.

Another breath in and feel your upper legs relaxing.

Release breath slowly

Breathe in, feel your hips relaxing.

Let it out

Breathe in, feel your torso, your tummy and chest relaxing.

Breathe out.

Breathe in, feel your shoulders relaxing.

Breathe out.

Breathe in, feel your arms relaxing.

Breathe out.

Breathe in, feel your hands relaxing.

Breathe out

Breathe in, feel your head relaxing. Clear your mind. Hear the silence.

Breathe out

Breathe normally now and continue to listen.

Concentrate on your breathing.

As you inhale, think and breathe in peace and love.

As you exhale, breathe out any negative thoughts.

Breathe in—peace and love

Breathe out—daily stresses
Breathe in—peace and love
Breathe out unwanted thoughts.
Be aware of your breathing now.
Inhale
Exhale and continue breathing normally.
Clear your mind.
Your mind is quiet. Your mind is clear.
Feel the presence of spirit as you listen to the silence.
Be at peace with your higher self. Be at peace with God.
You're safe here. Stay Relaxed.
You're now within; you now have attuned to spirit.

Become aware of the spirit world and as you keep daily activities and sounds out, focus on what's happening within your mind that doesn't involve daily life situations.

Stay within for 15 minutes.

(When you record the meditation leave a 15 minute gap with the water in the small fountain running for background sound and then speak again softly, saying)

Time is now up.

(And say this prayer followed by the remainder to complete this meditation)

(Prayer)

Great Divine Spirit, thank you for your protection.
Thank you for the contacts we've been given and
may your protection remain with us. Amen

Wiggle your feet back and forth.
Turn your hands over and rub them on your upper legs.
Bring yourself back.
Open your eyes.
Come back to reality.
Become aware of your surroundings.

(Now, discuss your experiences with your friends and if you're alone make notes so that you can reflect back. This will show you how well you did with future progression.)

No. 2: Meditation Explained

Listen and follow this visualization meditation until you gain control of your ability to calm your mind well on your own with the music of your choice, the running fountain or in silence, which meditation is recommended.

After you have achieved number two the next thing you should do is to visualize and create your own serene environment. Make it a place all your very own where you go each time for inner peace before you try to make a spirit contact. When you get there you'll feel a connection with God. This divine presence of spiritual energy brings love and peace and it will also enable you to make contact with your spirit guide.

Until you create your own personal quiet place you may use my special meadow, where there's a beautiful Rose Garden all around it.

Some teachers won't go through the process of talking you into a contact. I was told that my spirit guide would show me the way; to me that explanation wasn't acceptable. Once I discovered how to make contact with my guides and learned how to create I taught this to the people who sat in my home circle. This always worked well for them and it will for you. Let me take you there so you'll experience my guidance and then you'll have a better idea on how you can create your own place of peace.

This meditation will introduce you to a spiritual contact. This contact will be for one of your friends sitting and meditating with you; or if you're alone then it will be for you or someone that you know. Don't be so quick to relate any messages that will backfire as not all believe in a spirit world and connecting with it. The messages at the beginning will be short but they'll become longer as you progress and practice. When you do get a message from spirit ask who is giving it to you. You'll get a sense of whom it is. Visualize in your mind if it's a male or a female, aunt or uncle, mother or father, grandmother or grandfather, old or young, teenager, small child or an infant, tall or short, thin or heavy set, colour of hair and any other descriptions you may pick up such as a cause of death. You may also feel the presence of a pet. If at first you have a problem getting a message from spirit use psychic symbolic messages. What I mean by that is that you visualize an object or a gift for the individual you're focusing on and then give it to them in a message and interpret what it would mean. Such as if you see an airplane, (this to me would mean a trip,) then feel and sense if this trip is a needed one and encourage this person to take it as a trip usually means that one needs to get away from things to relax and take time for them self.

If you're sitting alone and make a contact, listen to what this spirit has to say. Like I said, this will most likely be a personal message or for a relative, maybe a friend that needs to hear this information. Get as much as you can and give it with love once you get an approval. Here again I like to stress the importance of having a friend or two to develop with and remember if you do get a message to give, always ask their permission to relate it to them. Example, mention their name if it is someone you know, ask the person if you don't know their name, saying, *"May I come to you?"* That is the polite and professional way.

If they say no then don't give, go on with your next message, don't take it personal. If they say yes then give the message and leave them with Gods blessing by saying, *"I leave it with you, God bless,"* for God has blessed them with a spiritual contact. Remember, never give a negative message or a message you wouldn't wish to receive yourself.

You'll be in silence for 5 minutes, and then you'll be spoken to again to guide you towards a spiritual contact, if you haven't already. But remember when you have a conversation with the spirit world it feels like you're having a conversation with yourself. Proof of spirit communication is in the message that's brought forth.

No. 2: Visualization Meditation

Relaxation should now come with ease if you followed number one to your comfort level.

Sit in a comfortable chair.

Rest your lower arms and hands on your upper legs, with the palms facing up.

Close your eyes and listen carefully.

Visualize the tube of light coming through the ceiling covering you and surrounding you with God's protection then grounding you as you did so often in number one. Relax your total body and clear your mind.

(Prayer)

> *Great Divine Spirit, protect us with your Infinite White Light. Guide us as we go within to communicate with spirit. Keep all evil entities*

away; give us your protection while we're on our
spiritual journey of meditation. Amen

Take a deep breath in and hold it—now—release it and slowly exhale.

Take another breath in, hold it—and slowly exhale.

Continue to focus on you breathing for a while as you breathe normally,—in—out—in—out—in—out.

Your breathing will become much slower as you relax and go deeper within.

Imagine yourself walking on an old cobblestone road in a beautiful tropical environment. The air is pleasantly warm and you feel a slight breeze coming from the ocean. Look in the distance, to your right and see a path with tall evergreen trees on both sides.

Walk towards it.

Enter the path through the trees and smell how sweet and fresh the air is.

Look ahead a short distance and you'll see the sun breaking thought them.

There's a ray of sunlight filtering through and shimmering on the green branches.

You'll gradually feel the warmth touch your face as you come from the shade.

There's a low stonewall just in front of you, it's about knee high, turn around and sit down on it.

Swing your legs in over and stand on the other side.

Lift your head and look in front of you.

There's a beautiful meadow surrounded with rose bushes that are all in bloom. You'll notice as you look around that there's a few large rocks scattered about with the many varieties of different shades of green grasses.

There are several patches of daylilies of different colours as if they have grown wild with the wild flowers.

Take a moment to notice the bright orange, yellows, and reds and smell the aroma that's all around you.

Turn your head slowly to the right and see the rose bushes lining that side of the meadow, as a hedge.

Walk over to the first pink rose, bend down and smell how beautiful it is. You'll feel the scent travel deep into your lungs and you know that it's a gift from God.

The rose bush next to it is a deep red.

Take a look down that side of the meadow, across the back hedge and look back up the other side.

Take notice of all the different colours of roses that God has created and presented to you.

Go and sit comfortably on one of the big stones in the meadow or sit back on the wall to begin your journey of spiritual contact.

Imagine a white dome covering this meadow and protecting you. This whole meadow is surrounded with roses and covered with God's protection of White Light.

Here's a place where you're safe from any harm.

Gods love and light is all around you now.

Your Spirit Guide just came and sat down by your side to guide you along the way. Rely on him and ask for assistance when you feel you need help.

Now; within your peaceful mind become aware of all your senses and recognize any contact that may come to you. When it presents itself, your awareness will stimulate your mind so that you may start to have a conversation with this spirit.

As you sit in silence let telepathic communication commence between you and your spiritual contact. Remember—your spirit guide is always with you. Be at peace and communicate. I'll speak with you again in 5 minutes.

(Give up to five minutes silence and then speak softly saying)

5 minutes are up now but stay within and remain calm and peaceful.

Let your mind be taken by your guide to a person meditating with you.

Direct your energy to them and feel it in their vibration. Feel yourself as one with him or her.

Telepathically ask spirit for a message.

Notice any images, pictures and scenery.

Visualize what spirit is sending forth and etching on your mind.

Listen to what is being said; look at what's being presented to you.

Ask your guide questions.

Use your imagination, sense as well as visualize.

If you see a colour or a flower, use it in your message as well.

Create from what you see, feel, and sense.

Imagine what it all means to you.

The meaning you create in your mind is quite often the interpreted message meant for the person you focused on?

Listen to your inner self and your inner thoughts; it's there within that you'll get your answers.

Those thoughts and answers are coming from the God source.

Stick with your first impressions.

(Remember, in this meditation you need to visualize in your mind a spirit entity and with much practise you'll see the spirit clairvoyantly without meditating)

When you feel you have a complete message, ask who gave it to you. Listen for a description and ask how this spirit is related to your message bearer. Once you've gotten all the answers direct your vibration to another.

Go through the same procedure.

Try not to forget your first message.

Stack your messages for now as you're a new beginner but eventually you won't need to.

Go ahead create.

I'll bring you back in *5 or 10* minutes.

(After the next *5 or 10* minutes speak softly saying)

Your time is now up.

Wiggle your feet back and forth.

Turn your hands over and rub them gently on your upper legs.

Bring yourself back.

Open your eyes.

Come back to reality.

Become aware of your surroundings.

(Prayer)

> *Great Divine Spirit, thank you for your protection. Thank you for the contacts we've been given and may your protection remain with us. Make us more knowledgeable each day and lead us safely on our spiritual journey. Amen*

Share your experience and give your messages.

No. 3: Guardian Meditation Explained

We're all assigned a guardian prior to our birth. This personal angel, your guardian, actually volunteered to be with you and remain with you throughout your earth life. This Guardian could very well be a distant family member who had passed long before your birth. He or she will be there to guide you towards the light when your life on earth ends. This moment we call death is but a new adventure into the next realm of existence known as the spirit world.

You may have had feelings of someone around you or felt someone of spirit close to you at times during your life. You can rest assured that it has been a Guardian or a loved one visiting to make them self known. Loved ones tend to do this when they know you need that special contact or affirmation of their existence. This will always remain with you throughout your material life. Such as a special scent, a special song, a special flower, a special poem or a feeling of longing to see them, the list could go on. This will be mostly what you'll experience. This happens mostly when you're alone and feel a need or long for comfort. You'll feel that special love emitting to you and you'll wonder what it's all about. You start to question yourself about those feelings and what you had actually experienced.

Guardians tend to guide you on the straight and narrow path. They'll alert you in danger through your intuition. Be there when you falter and help pick you up. Give you insight and answers to many unexplained situations and personal events happening in your life.

We all have freedom of choice and sometimes we go against our guardians. They won't ever desert you and will be there to help you bounce back when you make a decision against his or her advice. All you have to do is take a moment and go within and rely on them. Seek out the guidance you need and follow their advice; this will appear as if it's mainly your own intuition. You won't go wrong when it's given with love, received with love and directed with peace, love and harmony.

This meditation will introduce you to the one that has taken on the great task of watching over you and being by your side throughout your life, your guardian. Be alert as one of my students met her spirit guide during the visualization meditation and met her guardian in the spirit guide meditation, for some unknown reason. Be aware that your guardian could certainly be a distant relative that had passed through the veil quite sometime prior your birth, and your spirit guide will be someone unrecognizable.

No. 3: Meet Your Guardian Meditation

Sit and make yourself comfortable. Be aware of your inner self and don't fall asleep. As you go within your higher self you'll meet that special guardian who has volunteered with love and who has devoted an earth life existence, being a special angel to you.

(Prayer)

Dear God, our universal light of love and peace.

Thank you for giving me a special guardian to watch over and care for me throughout my lifetime. Bring my personal angel into my sight so we may finally meet face to face for a better understanding of each other. Bring my guardian with love and I will greet him or her also with love and endearment of appreciation. Amen

Sit comfortably and place your hands on your upper legs with the palms facing up.

Visualize the light of God coming through the ceiling as a big tube. Let it enter over the top of your head. Down around your shoulders and covering your upper body. Let it descend down around your torso, covering your legs and feet. Visualize it going through the floor and deep into mother earth, grounding you. As this had been put into motion you've now made contact with God. You're surrounded by his protection of white light and grounded to mother earth.

You are safe…

Let yourself be ready to meet your special guardian.

Take in a deep breath. (Counting silently 'in your mind' 1 2 3 4 5)

Let it out. (Count silently again 1 2 3 4 5)

Breathe in and say 'Guardian' in your mind.

Release it, exhaling all negative thoughts.

Take in another breath 'Guardian' 1 2 3 4 5

Release it and keep your mind clear 1 2 3 4 5

Breathe in, say 'Guardian' 1 2 3 4

Release it, say 'Guardian' 1 2 3 4

Breath normally now.

Visualize yourself all alone walking towards a park. You're walking on a well worn beaten-down path that has been used for centuries.

Go towards the entrance. Take notice that there's no gate to keep God's animal life outside.

Go through the entrance and you'll see a big old oak tree on your left. Stop and take a look at it, admire its strength and beauty. Look at the acorns; they're about ready to fall.

Listen to the silence.

(Pause momentarily)

You now hear the soft flutter of wings behind you.

Turn around and look at the Beautiful White Dove landing on one of the big oak trees magnificent branches that's close to the ground.

This beautiful bird of peace has come to guide you to your guardian.

Look at it and admire its purity.

You recognize each other. You feel a sense of protection; God's love and security is with you.

This beautiful bird flies to the next tree.

You now understand that it will lead you to your guardian.

Follow it and walk slowly and peacefully towards it.

Now, look down to your right and see the beautiful purple daisy like asters lining the edge of the path.

You hear the gentle flow of water from the small stream running along side.

The dove lands on the path ahead of you and walks a short distance waiting for you to catch up.

You can hear the beautiful sound of bird's singing and the cricket's chirping happily.

Look in the distance and see the ducks flying in to a pond that's up ahead.

You're nearing the dove now and it flies off again but remains in your vision.

Continue to follow; it's in no rush so please take your time.

You see an opening ahead and yes, there is a small pond.

You get a feeling of wonderment as you see the natural stone seats encircling it.

Take a look at the two beautiful white swans with their young, swimming gracefully together.

You're still aware of the dove; it's close by.

It flies and lands on a stone seat.

It looks back at you, beckoning you to come and sit in this particular spot; then it flies and lands on the ground nearby.

Walk over and sit down. You find it amazingly comfortable. The shape is well worn from the many uses.

Once again, look at the graceful swan's swimming.

Now, hold out your hand with an open palm.

The dove comes and lands on it momentarily.

It now spreads its wings once again and flies off in the opposite direction.

Sit quietly and wait; enjoy the peace and tranquility of the silence.

(Pause momentarily)

You hear the stream in the distance, the crickets chirping and the birds singing happily all around you.

You wait in anticipation.

Listen to the sounds around you right now.

(Pause and give a moment or two here)

The dove is now returning. You hear a gentle cooing and the fluttering sound of its wings.

With that you hear the quiet sound of chimes followed by beautiful classical music in the distance. You listen and appreciate this heavenly sound; you know you have never heard such beautiful music on earth.

The music lowers and you see the shape of a person coming from the distance following the same dove as you had.

This will be your Guardian.

Don't try to see yet but visualize in your mind what this guardian would look like.

Feel—whether it's a man or a woman.

Your guardian is arriving and requests that you keep looking at the swans until you've been given permission to meet.

You're anxiety arises and your heart is filled with love and excitement.

Now, feel the closeness of your guardian.

The dove comes and lands on the seat next to you.

You feel a loving vibration as the gap between you grows smaller.

You feel the strong energy.

It's a feeling of bliss; it's wonderful and loving.

A florescent cloud envelops both of you. You feel its magnificence and see its luminous vapour. The brightness is awesome and you sense that God's protection has gotten much stronger.

The dove leaves. It flies away and out of sight.

Your guardian sits by your side and takes your hand.

Feel, sense and visualize your guardian there.

Your excitement rises but you continue to look at the swans.

You feel the tenderness, gentleness and love as you're both sitting quietly together.

Now, you have permission;

Turn your head slowly around.

Look at this beautiful face.

This is your Guardian.

(Pause a moment or two for the reunion.)

Feel the presence of God with you.

Prepare yourself to leave this serene place.

The dove has now returned to guide you back.

Proceed to walk and notice that the trip back is much faster then it was going.

Start walking and follow the dove back down the path.

Listen to the sound of the crickets and the birds singing; notice that the sound is fading and is now in the background.

Notice the wild asters again and the sound of the peaceful flowing stream.

You no longer hear the crickets and the birds.

Take another look at the magnificent old oak tree and its acorns, as you pass by.

The dove is now bidding you farewell; its job is complete.

Exit the park and remain holding your guardians hand.

As you both leave this unspoiled beauty behind, you have a feeling of great inner peace.

Return safely back to your reality of consciousness and bring your guardian with you.

Now; Release the hand that you were holding.

Your guardian will always remain by your side.

(Prayer)

Great God, our infinite divine spirit of the universe. Thank you for your protection while you introduced me to my guardian. I'll listen to the advice and I'll follow the guidance given to me by my special angel. Amen.

Place your hands together and rub them gently back and forth. Now rub them gently on your upper legs and feel the energy being returned to you.

Come back slowly to reality.

Open your eyes.

Bring yourself back.

Bring yourself back now.

You now have met your Guardian. Discuss any results you've had with your friends involved.

God Bless you.

No.4: Spirit Guide Meditation Explained

You should be well able to go into a deep meditation at this point. You've had lots of practice from the past three so with little effort you'll go within your inner-self very easily. If you haven't followed the past three meditations as you should and haven't gotten completely through them, then you're still not ready for this one.

If you've successfully done and accomplished them, then…

Let me take you on a pleasant journey. This will be of the utmost importance and most beneficial as an introduction to your Spirit Guide.

You may have to go through this meditation several times before they are willing to show themselves. You might just be fortunate and spiritually developed enough to meet on the very first try.

Once again I remind you to have someone tape your meditations so that you will follow them with ease. It's impossible to meditate when you're reading unless you have years of practise. Please try this meditation only once a day. Do not repeat this twice in one session, as you'll be forcing them to make a choice they know you're not totally prepared for.

No. 4: Meeting Your Spirit Guide Meditation

Sit comfortably in a chair, lie down or sit in a lotus position. Just make yourself comfortable in a place where you don't fall asleep.

Close your eyes.

Rest your hands on your upper legs, palms up. Relax them and make them comfortable. Feel the tingling in your fingers and hands. This is energy from your guides. If you feel this energy, rub your hands gently together as friction will create an even more energized pulsation. Now, place your opened hands on your upper legs, palms down. Rub them gently back and forth about 3 or 4 times, giving that extra energy, back to you. Turn your hands over again, palms up, resting them on your upper legs

Now visualize a tube of white light coming through the ceiling, covering you and surrounding you with Gods protection. It's grounding you as it goes deep into mother earth.

Relax your total body and clear your mind.

(Prayer)

> *Our heavenly Father of divine intelligence. Guide us on our spiritual journey. Keep us safe with the protection of your white light as we go within our higher selves. Guide us onward to meet our long awaited Spirit Guide. Make our meeting pleasant and peaceful as we finally come in contact with each other for the first time. Amen*

Let's begin your journey.

Take in a deep breath and hold it. 1—2—3—4—5

Now...Let it out and hold. 1—2—3—4—5

Release it and continue breathing normally

Listen to my voice and only to my voice, block out all other noises.

Take a breath in—let your mind say…'Spirit Guide.'

Breathe out—rid your mind of any other thoughts.

Deep breath in…'Spirit guide.'

Breathe out all other thoughts and negativity.

Clear your mind.

Deep breath in…'Spirit guide.'

Breathe out. Keep your mind clear.

Now focus entirely on your Spirit Guide.

Breathe In….'Spirit guide.'

Breathe out…'Spirit guide.'

Your mind is totally focused on your spirit guide.

You're standing in a field of rich green grass, which is very unusual for this climate.

It's spring and the daisies are in bloom. The field is covered with a beautiful mass of white, as white as freshly fallen snow. Look at all the flowers and admire their beauty.

There's a mountain in front of you.

Start walking slowly towards the big rock boulders in front of it.

This place looks familiar; you've been here before.

You know it's safe.

You hear a cry of an eagle. It's flying overhead and watching you.

Look at it; take notice of the pure white of her head and tail.

She's circling above and beckoning you to follow the trail that's leading into the mountain.

You obey and start walking.

You begin to climb.

Slowly and comfortably you continue on your journey.

Look to your right and see a beautiful tall pine tree that's about a century old. It's bark thick and hard, ruffed and ragged from the harsh winters.

You stop to admire it and continue walking.

You're feeling rather energetic as you continue to climb.

Up and up you go.

Watch out for the pieces of fallen branches and the stones in the pathway.

Keep walking.

You're coming upon another trail now; it's like a crossroads.

There's a beautiful white wolf sitting in the centre.

You remember him from your last visit and he recognizes you.

He's waiting. He's staring at you with his hypnotic piercing yellow eyes.

See him—in your mind.

Don't be afraid, he's your guide and protector along the way.

Walk towards him and feel his strength and energy.

He's motionless. You walk closer.

You're standing in front of him now and you can see how bright and beautiful his eyes actually are.

You approach him.

He stands at attention and you telepathically greet each another.

You reach out and touch his head and feel the thickness of his coat.

Take your hand away and offer the back of it for him to smell.

He gently lifts his head and licks it. You feel the warm moisture from his tongue. You feel the wetness of his nose.

He turns and takes the path to your left that leads to your destination.

Follow him.

It's a steep climb, but continue.

You follow him and admire his strength. He's very sure of his step and it never falters.

You know he's taking you where you have to go.

Continue to follow.

The eagle is still watching from above.

Listen, there's a few loose stones falling down the grade behind you.

You hear them as they roll away.

Keep your step. Don't look back.

Up and up you go.

You're a fair distance up the mountain now.

You feel a little tired, but you're almost there.

Take a moment—stop and turn around.

Look at the beauty in front of you.

Notice in the distance how the dry climate has made a barren land with a few huge trees. There's a small lake and some wild horses. A passing wagon is creating a lot of dust in the sandy dry soil.

Now, turn back again and proceed upward.

Continue to follow that magnificent animal. Up you go.

He's a little ahead of you now.

He slows down.

You reach him and continue your journey.

Now, look ahead, see a clear level area with patches of dry grass and a few small rocks in the near distance.

The wolf stands at attention.

He's very alert, his ears and face are pointing forward.

He's staring intently.

You move slowly toward him. You see the back of someone looking in the other direction; looking out over the barren land. The eagle is perched on his or her shoulder.

Don't try to see who it is yet.

It's a beautiful scene. You're feeling very peaceful and spiritual. You feel a loving connection with your guide.

Within moments your difficult climb will be well worth the effort.

You move closer.

Move a little closer.

Feel and sense the excitement.

The eagle leaves. She flies high above—calling loudly.

The wolf now walks you towards your guide.

Follow him.

Don't try to see your guide just yet.

Now, visualize in your mind what your guide will probably look like from what you've already seen.

You're approaching; your heart begins to beat faster with anticipation. You're anxious but yet slightly afraid. You feel the desire to run forward, also to run away.

You walk closer now; you're getting very near and you smell a familiar scent. Your guide is now aware of you. Your guide is patiently waiting.

Go closer—go on—closer.

The wolf nuzzles your guides' shoulder and then moves away.

Now—reach down and touch the same shoulder.

Your guide is slowly turning around—to greet you.

Look—at this magnificent face.

(Take a moment to visualize and see your guides face.)

Pause a moment to greet each other.

This is your spirit guide that's currently with you and you finally meet.

Take a good look and remember.

Ask for a name, you may be presented with one but if you're not then it will be presented to you in time.

God blesses you with you Spirit Guide companion.

Take a moment to get acquainted.

Pause a moment.

Your guide stands up and takes your hand.

You both turn and begin to descend down the mountain.

Start walking down now.

You have your guide by your side.

The wolf is ahead—leading the way.

The eagle flies and watches from above. She calls out—cries of joy.

Down you go.

You sense a beautiful feeling of elation.

Watch out for the stones and the dead branches in the pathway.

Stop and take another look at the wild horses and the barren land.

The trip back is much faster as it's downhill.

Down you go

You're now at the crossroads.

You past them—look back and notice the paths are disappearing as you leave them behind.

Down and down you go taking each step cautiously.

You see the exit from the mountain.

Now; you're passing the big old pine tree. You smell its scent as you pass by.

You're now at the big rock boulders, at the bottom.

Your journey is complete.

Stay within until I bring you back.

You now have your Spirit Guide hand in hand with you. Rely on your guide, the wolf and the eagle.

They're with you always—when you need them.

Call on them. They're there for you.

Once again focus on your breathing.

Breathe in…1—2—3—4—5

Breathe out…1—2—3—4—5

Breathe normally now.

Stay within.

(Prayer)

> *Thank you—Great Infinite Spirit—for introducing my Spirit Guide. I'll use my guide wisely as I'm on my spiritual path to help make contact with those whom I seek. Amen*

Turn your hands over and gently rub them on your upper legs.

And open your eyes.

Open your eyes.

Bring yourself forward.

Bring yourself back.

Bring yourself back…Now

Move around in your chair and become aware of your surroundings.

(Talk and discuss any of your experiences with your friends and circle members.

One at a time gives the other person a chance to have their say.)

God Bless you.

Epilogue

The original title for this book was going to be MACED, with the now title *Psychic Ability, Clairvoyance Powers* at the bottom of the cover page. I saw and understood the meaning of MACED. Once evaluated I decided to change it because it gave negative connotations even with an explanation; the title of a book needs to give the reader a definition and an idea of the contents held within, basically explaining what the book is all about.

Below is this explanation.

Mace as per Webster's dictionary says that it comes from 14th century Old French, from assumed Vulgar Latin mattia, meaning a heavy, often spiked, staff or club used as a weapon especially in the Middle Ages for breaking armour, an ornamental staff borne as a symbol of authority before a public official or a legislative body, an aromatic spice consisting of the dried external fibrous covering of a nutmeg that is used as a temporarily disabling liquid usually used as a spray, referred to as Pepper Spray.

Either one of the above used on you would put you out of this life for a short period or forever, depending on the force, authority given and the amount used.

I chose this name because once you learn to grasp an **Attunement** with spirit, you get **Enlightened**. Once enlightened your **Development** begins and then it will enhance the power of **Clairvoyance**. Once you see clairvoyantly you have the insight needed to have mediumistic powers. Therefore when combining all four of those together it puts you in the category of having **Mediumship** abilities.

Taking the first letter from **M**ediumship, **A**ttunement, **C**lairvoyant, **E**nlightenment and **D**evelopment gives you the title that makes the word **MACED.**

Imagine yourself being maced by the police using pepper spray.

When you're dealing with Clairvoyance and Mediumship you're dealing with Spirit. You're venturing out of this world. When you get maced with pepper spray, you're probably dealing with crime. This spray will also put you out of this world, but in a more unpleasant way. Both results are totally different. When dealing with mediumship the results are very pleasant and uplifting with contact from a deceased loved one in his/her new realm of existence. When being maced with pepper spray you become disorientated and totally out of your existence, as you've known it prior to the attack; burning eye's causing temporary blindness, disorientation, dizziness, vertigo and shock being the end results. You're also out of this world without the loving contact from the other side.

Precognition, psychokinetic, materialization and levitation are also some of the things that may be of interest to you as you learn, practice and grow towards a higher energy; this will come from an interest to develop further, when you're ready. You'll find that other unexplained happenings will attract your attention as you continue and progress at a natural pace. Keep in mind that you get from it what you need and what you want. As you continue your journey of developing your clairvoyance you'll progress through enlightenment.

We all know what it's like to advance from one grade to another from school days; psychic awareness, clairvoyance and mediumship are the same. From the time of our understandings of growth and self progression we're aware of intuition, often known as 'gut feeling'. Some of you may remember a voice once heard in your inner ear or had seen a ghost or apparition of some sort. Connecting clairvoyantly is a derivative of this, such as from one grade to another. Often times one is in need of a good development teacher for platform work in guidance of presentation as it gives reassurance of competency.

This book is but a beginners guide to help access you in the direction of a self inner-search for God on your journey from psychic to clairvoyance. It'll lead you to gain that ability to make direct contact with the spirit world that consists of great love that's there and has always been there for you. Believe in yourself and recognize your capabilities. Search within your subconscious mind to make such a contact and recognize the God source as always being there to assist you in your endeavours. Watch for a sequel to this book.

Love and light continuous.

J.A. Brown

If interested:

Go to the Web Site below to find a Spiritualist Church near you.

http://www.lighthousespiritualcentre.ca/Churches/
churchcanada.html#ONTARIO

For a wonderful teacher and a gifted medium check out Rev.
Dr. Alva Folkes website www.alvafolkes.com or the website
for her church www.fosc.ca

All are welcome.

About the Author

J.A. Brown is a Canadian citizen residing in Scarborough, Ontario, Canada. He was born February 17th 1952. He has one daughter and one grand daughter and they bring tremendous joy to his life. He has a love of animals and nature. He spends many hours in the great outdoors and meditates in his beautiful garden as he listens to the sound of soft running water from the fountain in the centre of the small man-made pond. He feeds the birds so there are a lot of birds singing while he does. He holds a great respect for the universe and all that it consists of. His passion for understanding God has escalated over the past 20 years and he's working on becoming an ordained minister here in Toronto, Canada and in Britain, UK. He gets a lot of information from the spirit world as he's able to make such a contact. There are times when he has to shut them out because of the amount of chatting in his ears.

I've known him for over twenty years. We used to go to a friend's cottage and that included my mother, who was then well into her eighties. Jerry known as Joe, which he prefers, being in the medical profession knew just how to help her and his helping gave me the respite that I needed; into the boat en route to the cottage, out of the boat, up a very difficult hilly path and so on. I learnt that he is not only compassionate and capable but he is also in tune with nature, spotting birds resting on the surface of the lake as only his natured trained eyes could. The rest of us seldom saw them unless they flew away!

I gradually learnt too that water birds were not the only thing of which he was aware and of which the rest of us were in blissful ignorance. He had to be psychic and clairvoyant. I used to listen to his stories, usually told only to me because he knew I believed in him.

Recently he has had more time to devote to his spiritual growth and all that it entails. Along with this he has a facility with words that's quite phenomenal. Compassion has not left him either. Like I said, he has joined the ministry and hoping to be ordained in the near future. He has recently become the Associate Minister at The Fellowship of Spiritualists' Church in Oshawa, Ontario, Canada. He's always there to lend a hand, guiding his students through choppy waters and is selfless in his giving.

I hope you will enjoy this book and his unique way of expressing things.

Margaret Young.

This book is written for an individual or groups of people who would like to learn from its contents and meditations. The context and its meditations are not written for skeptics but for a person in need of soul searching and learning more about life on the other side. The chapters are short, condensed, intense and very informative; they are not filled with a lot of nothingness. It contains straight to the point information to give you the awareness needed for a better understanding of your psychic gift and inner connections with the God source.

What you read and learn from here are personal experiences I've had over a period of years. Now I share them with you so you'll be capable of reaching spirit by going within to find that contact which you so desire. This is a beginner's guide written in a simple format, easily understood and it's also an introduction to Spiritualism. It's written in a way that I would like to have found when I was a beginner. Personally I feel there are great Mediums out there but they have not yet put their teachings on paper. I too continue to learn each day and keep an open mind for a greater understanding of spirit.

For the reader who doesn't have an interest in developing his skills, the information and true ghost stories will provide you with enlightenment. As you continue to read let the subconsciousness of your mind be the judge of any inner feelings dealing with an afterlife. Your intuitive knowingness will provide you with a positive aspect of immortality.